A HANDWRITING MANUAL

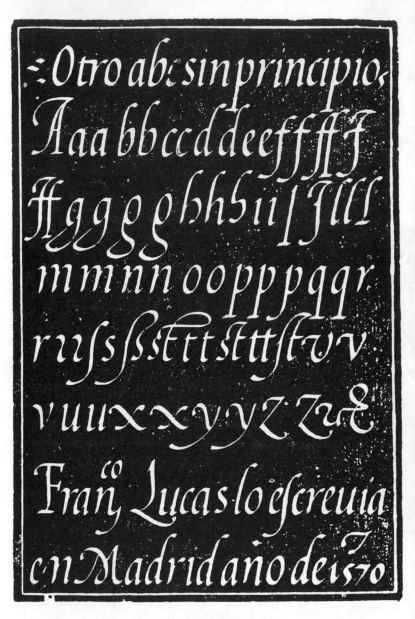

From Arte de escrivir *by Francisco Lucas. Madrid,* 1577

A
HANDWRITING
MANUAL

by

ALFRED FAIRBANK

faber and faber
LONDON · BOSTON

Published by the Dryad Press in 1932
First published by Faber and Faber Limited
3 Queen Square, London WC1
in a new and enlarged edition in 1954
Second impression 1956
Third edition revised and enlarged 1961
First published as a Paperback Edition 1965
Reprinted 1968
Revised and enlarged edition 1975
Reprinted 1978 and 1983
Printed in Great Britain by
Whitstable Litho Ltd., Whitstable, Kent
All rights reserved

ISBN 0 571 04867 6

To

J. R. F.

'Now any spiritual elevation must come through competent teachers cultivating the idea of Beauty in the young. That children have an innate love of Beauty is undeniable. Yet this is so little recognized that our best and most attentive teachers frequently exhibit surprise when they discover a greater aesthetic sensibility in their young pupils than in the mature intelligence of their own inculcated minds; and they will even take credit for this acute observation. But, while the intellectual faculty is still dormant, spiritual things are to children as music is, which a child readily absorbs, without thought, although a full-grown man, if he has lacked that happy initiation, can scarcely by grammar come at the elements.'

From a broadcast lecture 'Poetry' by Robert Bridges given on February 28, 1929.

AUTHOR'S NOTE TO THE NINTH EDITION

A series of new illustrations have been added to this edition showing demonstration scripts written by a number of accomplished writers in England, U.S.A. and Canada. These make a remarkable and valuable feature of this edition, for they give evidence of the international usefulness of italic handwriting, as well as of its various expressions of grace. The comments on handwriting in the examples add further to the value of the book.

Most of the examples come from America and represent the rising attention now being given to the virtues of italic handwriting in several States of the U.S.A. More control will have been used by the contributors than would be appropriate for scribbled notes which would stress individuality rather than style and legibility, and therefore would not fit the educational purpose of this book. This is not to say that the italic hand restricts casual usage, such as in making hasty memoranda, shopping lists, and other ephemera, for it is an all-purposes style.

An interesting circumstance which has arisen of late is that versions of my simple italic alphabet of Figure 40 have been published in the U.S.A., Sweden and East Germany. The simplicity of this alphabet and the fact that it can be easily developed into fluent writing, entitles it as worthy of study by educational authorities concerned with the teaching of the young.

ALFRED FAIRBANK

February 1974

ACKNOWLEDGEMENTS

Grateful acknowledgements for permission to use copyright material or for assistance are made as follows: To the Director of the British Museum, the Director of the Victoria & Albert Museum, the Vice-Prefect of the Biblioteca Apostolica Vaticana, the Deputy Keeper of the Public Record Office, the Curator of the Colchester and Essex Museum, and Mr Frank Allan Thomson, for permission to reproduce Renaissance manuscripts. To the Trustees of the Conrad Estate and Messrs J. M. Dent for permission to use extracts from the writings of Joseph Conrad for the display of examples. To the Literary Trustees of Walter de la Mare, and the Society of Authors for permission to use *The Horseman* by Walter de la Mare, and to John Lane (Bodley Head) and the author W. B. Rands, for permission to reproduce the verse copied by Richard Yates-Smith. To the Dryad Press, Leicester, and Messrs Ginn & Co. Ltd. for permission to reproduce my exemplar examples from *Dryad Writing Cards* and *Beacon Writing Books*. To Air Chief Marshal Sir Theodore McEvoy, John Marsden and Jack Trodd, Misses Catharine Fournier and Anna Hornby for the fine specimens from their pens and also to Professor Lloyd Reynolds, Messrs Bruce Barker-Benfield, Alf Ebsen, Arthur L. Davies, James Hayes, Maury Nemoy, Paul Standard, Lewis Trethewey, Mesdames Barbara Getty, Margaret Horton, Jacqueline Svaren, Sheila Waters, and Miss Vera Law. To Messrs Denys John and Kenneth C. Yates-Smith (himself a writing master), and Misses Winifred Hooper and Vera Howells, for providing me with examples of children's handwriting.

The author was indebted to most distinguished and revered friends who have died: Sir Sydney Cockerell, Joseph Compton, Geoffrey Ebbage, and James Wardrop.

CONTENTS

A Handwriting Manual

ILLUSTRATIONS
IN THE TEXT

PLATES
FOLLOWING PAGE 94

21. Writing by a girl at a Barking School. 1938
22. Writing by a girl at a Barking School. 1938
23. Writing by Carole Basdell when aged 8
24. Writing by Barbara Fellows when aged 9
25. Writing by Dorothy Marks when aged 10
26. Writing by Carole Wells when aged 9
28. Writing by Carole Wells when aged 10
29. Writing by Carole Wells when aged 12
30. Writing by Jonathan Yates-Smith when aged 9
31. Wiriting by Richard Yates-Smith when aged 11
32. Part of a story written by Gillian Barnes when aged 10
33. Writing by Ian Ebbage when aged 12
34. Writing by Air Chief Marshall Sir Theodore McEvoy
35. Letter by Mr Joseph Compton, C.B.E
36. Letter by Mr J. S. T. Trodd
37. Letter by Mr John Marsden
38. Letter by Miss Catharine Fournier
39. Sonnet transcribed by Alfred Fairbank, 1936
40. Writing by Mrs Sheila Waters
41. Writing by Miss Vera Law
42. Writing by Mr Lewis Trethewey
43. Writing by Mr Paul Standard
44. Writing by Mr Maury Nemoy
45. Writing by Mr Bruce Barker-Benfield
46. Writing by Mrs Margaret Horton
47. Writing by Professor Lloyd Reynolds
48. Writing by Mr Alf Ebsen
49. Writing by Mr Arthur L. Davies
50. Writing by Mr James Hayes
51. Writing by Mrs Jacqueline Svaren
52. Writing by Mrs Barbara Getty
53. Writing by Mr Thomas Barnard

INTRODUCTION

Handwriting is a functional thing, intended for communicating and recording thought. It is to be read, and therefore legibility is an essential virtue. By also expressing personality it has a value that is appreciated by everybody: indeed there are some who seem to regard legibility as less important than the mark of individuality that handwriting bears. We may look for more in handwriting, however, for though it certainly should be legible and inimitable, it may also have the quality of the craftsman's work. How excellent that handwriting can provide an outlet for skill and aesthetic feeling, particularly where the ability to draw is lacking. How worth-while when handwriting interests the writer and pleases the reader. How satisfying when something ordinary and commonplace is raised towards the beautiful. Just as speech can be a delightful vehicle of words and thoughts, so too can handwriting; and so language is served.

The italic hand, with which this book is concerned, is one equally suitable for use by the young child at school and by the adult. The child needs a simple but practical and interesting system, whilst the reforming adult who is discontented with what his writing has become, and wishes for relief from the boredom of scribble, asks for a script that has grace as well as legibility and speed. So vital is the italic script that a Society for Italic Handwriting has been formed with an international membership.

Handwriting when considered as an art is calligraphy. Calligraphical principles and methods are put forward herein which, if applied, will produce a beautiful script that is also legible and capable of meeting the stresses of speed. Beauty is not a decorative external element which can be added to a script and thus transform it, so that it can then be called calligraphy.

Writing is performed by movements: it is a dance of the pen. When looking at handwriting we do not see the motions of the pen, but the trail of ink laid by the pen when it was in contact with paper. Yet a handwriting model which ignored the kind of motions involved in writing would be a poor guide. The line and shape of italic is an expression of movement.

The purpose of this book is to give instruction to the adult who is bent on reforming his handwriting or who is a teacher of children. It is assumed the teacher is generally in both these categories and will wish to write in the style he or she teaches. The best teacher of handwriting is obviously something of a penman himself, who knows what good writing is and how to write well. This is perhaps a hard saying, yet young children, being imitative, may be as much impressed by the movements they see when a teacher writes on a blackboard as by a static timeless exemplar written by a calligrapher unknown to them. Mrs Margaret Darrell has remarked: 'Good copybooks provide good models but, with children, good models do not necessarily provide good writers—good teachers are the link.'

In addition to teachers and amateurs there are those who are interested professionally in the design of lettering: namely, calligraphers, typographers, commercial artists, signwriters, etc. To these a knowledge of the italic letter and the principles governing its form and design are obviously desirable. Because italic lends itself to variety so much more than the Roman letter, the study of italic by letterers and printers is therefore of importance.

Although this manual was originally intended to do no more than put forward a system of handwriting for ordinary usage, the grace of italic has drawn attention to the possibilities and potential value of the set italic script for use for formal purposes and also as a special hand for those occasions when there is a desire to make and to please and when speed of execution is not a factor (*cf.* Plates 39 and 40). Edward Johnston once said to his pupils: 'When a thing is different it is not the same!' A set italic is not a 'precious' free italic: it is not the same. Normally, of course, the writer will want to move away from the set italic towards freedom and speed.

The instruction given here is in the writing of a careful copy-book hand in the italic style of the author's model. A model, of course, is not an indication of what the developed hand should resemble, for exemplars are written slowly and with precision, so as to make teaching clear and to indicate the desirable movements, and they need at first to be copied slowly. Models are better if they are pure calligraphy and do not show expressions of per-sonality. The idiosyncrasies of the writing-master need to be weeded since they serve no purpose. In point of fact, an exemplar should be exemplary (as far as possible!). Freedom and speed which come with practice after the initial study of the model naturally modify the script. In a sense, a model is but a guide to the beginning of an unknown personal journey, the directions one takes later being a matter of private inclination. In seeking direc-tion, self-tuition and self-criticism are most valuable. The Renais-sance scripts and models often have a quality greater than we have attained but which we should aim to secure. Reference to them as well as to the author's model is advised.

The model offered, therefore, is a set version of italic hand-writing in which are incorporated common characteristics of the humanistic cursives of the Renaissance and favours narrow curving bends rather than pointed angles. There are numerous versions of italic handwriting of the fifteenth and sixteenth centuries, but the model is not derived from any one source, though it is held to be essentially true italic. This manual was first published in 1932 and since then the system has been tried out sufficiently both by schools and by adults to be put forward with confi-dence. (The author has given lessons to quite 1,000 adults.) The common criticisms encountered are that the script is neces-sarily slow, and tends to preciousness and to the elimination of individuality. These criticisms, backed by insufficient knowledge, are certainly not accepted, and, in fact, are denied, but even if they were sound, nobody questions the high standard of legibility in reformed italic hands. The faster one writes the more individual is the writing. A child who is found to be writing italic too slowly is probably trying too hard. In the handwriting lessons painstaking practice is right, but away from them freedom must offset discipline. Discipline gives skill and freedom gives speed.

The sort of pen recommended for italic handwriting is one which makes thicks and thins naturally, has little flexibility, and is easy-running.

Speed in handwriting is achieved by personal ability, but there are many economies which can be effected and which are included in the model.

Rhythm, an essential to speed (though often hurtful to legibility), is inherent in many of the letters of the alphabet, and pattern comes simply and delightfully. There seems no end to the possible calligraphical graces of italic.

To write well one must wish to do so; and this points to the importance of teachers showing by their attitude a regard for this worth-while activity. Some teachers have remarked upon the improved morale of a class when handwriting has been taught with understanding. As the act of writing legibly imposes control and self-discipline it is not surprising that there should be some overlap. Also it has been noted that children brought to appreciate their lessons in penmanship often show an increased interest in other school subjects.

THE DEVELOPMENT OF ITALIC

When Florentine scholars, early in that period we know as the Italian Renaissance, began to search for the forgotten classic authors, they found manuscripts written in the carolingian (or caroline) minuscules of earlier centuries. The clear rounded letters appealed to the humanists and they adopted versions of it for their own use. By difference in the usage of the revived caroline script it became, on the one hand, the very legible, noble, and serene Roman letter of developed structure and formality, whilst on the other it grew into the fluent, elegant, and spirited italic, executed with a precision ranging from a copy-book standard to complete informality.

The invention of the Roman hand has been credited to Poggio Bracciolini and the italic hand to Niccolò Niccoli by Professor B. L. Ullman.

The humanistic cursives of the fifteenth century were at times rounded, in the style of the Caroline script, but later became narrower. The narrower letter was at first curvilinear but later sometimes pointed. Eventually the italic hand developed into the copperplate hand.

The qualities of clarity, speed, and grace of the italic hand were recognized in the Papal Chancery, where in the fifteenth century it began to be used for writing papal briefs. It became a hand of the courts, and letters to Henry VIII from France, Spain, Germany, Poland, etc., show that at that time the script was widely adopted abroad. Henry's children, Edward VI and Elizabeth, were taught the italic hand by Roger Ascham, himself a fine penman. Undoubtedly of the cursive hands there is none in Western history to equal the finest Renaissance examples, and this is generally recognized by calligraphers and typographers.

The first printed writing book to teach italic was printed in Rome in 1522 and was *La Operina* by Ludovico degli Arrighi (Vicentino), and the instruction was entirely given over to writing *lettera cancellarescha* (Fig. 36). This was followed by Arrighi's *Il Modo* (Venice, 1523) and showed *litera da brevi* and other scripts and alphabets (Plate 9). In England the first printed writing manual, *A Booke Containing Divers Sortes of Hands* by Jean de Beauchesne and John Baildon (London, 1571), gave an example of the *Italique hande* (Plate 19). There are many of the early writing manuals with exemplars printed from precisely engraved wood blocks preserved in our national libraries, of which those of Ludovico Arrighi, G. A. Tagliente, Gerard Mercator, G. P. Palatino, Casper Neff, Vespasiano Amphiareo, Juan de Yciar, G. F. Cresci, Francisco Lucas and Jean de Beauchesne are notable for their models of italic. In 1501 Aldus Manutius Romanus published in Venice the first of his famous series of classics printed throughout in a type which came to be named *italic* and the success of this venture in cheap production consolidated the position of the letter. Later, Arrighi also designed fine italic types that were used in their own right: i.e. without association with Roman.

abcdefghijklmnopqrstuvwxyz
'Monotype' Blado

abcdefghijklmnopqrstuvwxyz
'Monotype' Arrighi

abcdefghijklmnopqrstuvwxyz
'Monotype' Lutetia

abcdefghijklmnopqrstuvwxyz
'Monotype' Bembo

abcdefghijklmnopqrstuvwxyz
'Monotype' Narrow Bembo

FIG. I
Lower case italic alphabets used in book printing

Italic in printing, though not enjoying today the popularity it had in the early years of the sixteenth century when it was often used without association with Roman, is seen often enough to be perfectly legible. Its present employment by the printer is as a type supplementary to Roman for the purposes of differentiation or emphasis; that is, for prefaces, quotations, titles, foreign words, words to be stressed, etc., and the printer's slanting compressed letter certainly provides a contrast. Sometimes it is used for the printing of poetry because, though quite legible, it cannot be read with so much ease as Roman, and the slower pace of reading is appropriate to the less quickly apprehended verse. When the printer of a book has to print a letter to a correspondent he frequently uses italic, which tends to evoke the idea of handwriting. The slope of the italic types has often been excessive and this is excused by their contrasting function. The reader will note the slant of the sixteenth-century italic hands shown in this book is slight (*cf.* p. 53).

CHARACTERISTICS OF ITALIC

The primary and essential difference between italic and Roman hands of the Renaissance is not that italic is compressed and sloped, as in modern type, but that italic has developed through speed and is shaped by the greater tempo of execution. One effect of speed in handwriting can be indicated in illustration: there is time enough for the professional calligrapher writing a formal hand or for an infant writing print-script to make an 'm' with three (or more) strokes, but in more current writing there may not be time available to allow the pen to leave the paper, and so the *m* may be written with a continuous stroke. At once, as a

FIG. 2

result of the economy of strokes imposed by speed, the arches of the letter springing from a different point (from high up the stem

19

or arch in Roman and from the very base in italic) tend to change in form, and a differently shaped letter results.

The common features of the sixteenth-century cursive italic letter are: its relationship to Roman, freedom through speed, tendency to narrowness, slight slope to the right, simply executed serif or flourish, and sharp contrast of thick and thin strokes. But in a letter allowing a vast range of degrees of freedom and fluency, and evolved at a time when individuality in handwriting was finding full expression, it is not surprising that search produces many instances where freedom is restricted, or compression slight, or letters are upright, or a blunt pen has reduced natural gradation and contrast in thickness of strokes.

For the purposes of this manual it is of the first importance that italic is so formed that most letters may be joined readily by natural ligatures.

The elongation in the italic hands of the parts of letters going above or below the bodies, as in *d* and *p* (known respectively as 'ascenders' and 'descenders'), is a normal visual effect of lateral compression. A further corollary of the use of narrowed letters is that lines are well spaced; and in the ample spaces between the lines the ascenders and descenders, often flourished, present a pleasing contrast to the close patterning of the bodies of the letters and add a secondary pattern.

LEGIBILITY

Legibility is obviously the first essential virtue of handwriting. By legibility one generally means the clarity or readableness of print or script. Robert Bridges wrote in S.P.E. Tract No. XXIII ('English Handwriting') that 'True legibility consists in the *certainty of deciphering* and that depends not on what any one reader may be accustomed to, nor even on the use of customary forms, but rather on the consistent and accurate formation of the letters. For instance, it is a common fault even with good writers to write *n* and *u* exactly alike: a writer with this habit is so far illegible . . . the only qualification of this definition of true legibility is that social convenience has a full claim to respect, and the shapes of the letters should (for the sake of general legibility) conform sufficiently to accepted use; because, though this is a point of good manners rather than of good writing, it must be allowed as a factor of common practical legibility.'

To form letters as much alike as *n* and *u* or *r* and *v* with adequate precision, even when the pen is moving quickly, calls for skill. Practice makes perfect, but a careful attitude is also required.

There is a considerable range of legibility from (say) the excellence of the Roman text of this book (Monotype Aldine Bembo) to the hand which is difficult but possible to read; and indeed within this range there is a wide difference between a good handwriting and a base scribble. Since legibility depends so much upon what we are used to reading, it follows that I can read my own scribble with an ease others are unlikely to match. Robert Bridges remarked 'that those who are accustomed to bad writing find good writing difficult to read'. No careful and scientific measure of clarity therefore can be found and the only criterion can be *certainty of deciphering*.

For an alphabet which needs to have the quality of readableness the designer must make letters of simple, distinctive, and proportioned form; i.e., the letters must have no unnecessary parts, must not be the cause of confusion, and must not show exaggeration or dwarfing. The letter must have family likeness, be coordinated, be capable of harmonious and patterned spacing, and be of good shape. Nor should it be forgotten that the tops of letters have greater importance to the eye than the bottoms (see Fig. 3).

minim

FIG. 3

The movements that come most easily to the individual may not accord with those required by our alphabet and thus freedom may aid speed but control aids legibility.

BEAUTY

If legibility is difficult to assess in its varying conditions, how much more so is beauty. What is a good shape, a pure form, or a fine proportion? What is a good rhythmic flow, a graceful curvature, a harmony of patterning? Perhaps the answers to such awkward questions are best given obliquely; taste may be developed by acquaintanceship with the finest examples of handwriting, and beauty may be found as a by-product of right methods of penmanship.

A handwriting which has abstract beauty is not necessarily legible, for there is beautiful *bad* writing: a writing perhaps having a melodic flow and a quality of line and pattern but which is too undisciplined, too little related to traditional alphabets, or too free, to allow words to be read without difficulty.

In our appreciation of cursive calligraphy we may note the quality of paper and ink, the sensitive touch, the fine shapes and good proportions of letters, the graceful and firm curvature given by the flying pen, the adjustments of letters to make patterned words, and the arrangement of lines and margins on the sheet. There is also that expression of personality which emerges to our satisfaction in all handwriting. This, however, is not always a fortunate feature, but it is one we want, and indeed is inevitable, in italic as in any other system of cursive writing.

UNITY

In examining the finest examples of handwriting we know, one is impressed by a sense of unity (which includes orderliness, harmony, homogeneity, and neatness, and implies that the whole is made up of related parts). It is of some importance therefore to know that unity can be secured by:

(*a*) using a pen that gives consistent incidence of thickness, thinness, and gradation of strokes, when held in a consistent manner,

(*b*) a consistent pen-position,

(*c*) making letters proportionate to each other and by avoiding exaggeration or dwarfing of individual letters or parts of letters,

(*d*) maintaining consistent size and slope,

(*e*) making letters that mix well with each other: i.e. that have family relationship and likeness and the same fundamental rhythm,

(*f*) giving letters the appearance of being equally spaced in the words,

(*g*) using suitable joins,

(*h*) writing rhythmically and with fluency, and

(*i*) good alignment.

The writing of a good hand can be thought of as an exercise in the achievement of unity.

SPEED AND EXPEDIENCE

Many factors governing a speedy performance in handwriting are personal, for example, age, health, energy, mental ability, the hand, experience in writing, pace and precision attempted, pressures exerted by fingers and hand, size of writing, etc. There are also economies of movement and effort which can be arranged to help speed, such as simple, fluent, and rhythmic letter-forms, short joins, suitable pen lifts, easy-running pens comfortably held, etc. In designing the exemplar hand of this manual much consideration has been given to the avoidance of unnecessary effort, and labour-saving devices are incorporated.

Expedience relates to suitability, feasibility, and economy, as well as speed. It is not sensible for a child to be expected to write in a manner not suited to his age and development, nor for an adult to write his correspondence slowly and laboriously—unless he wishes to produce a result that can only come from the exercise of great care. If handwriting is to be thought of as a craft ('everyman's craft') then it is a practical matter. The young child who can only write slowly must be given, however, a model which is a preparation for the time when he will need to write quickly. This implies that a child should begin as it is intended he should go on.

FREEDOM AND CONTROL

Legibility is secured only by some self-discipline and control. The cursive hand of the adult should be one acquired by years of continuous skilful experience and good habits extending back to childhood. Even so when an adult writes he must keep 'half an eye' on the trail of ink proceeding from his pen and so he is never completely free from 'writing-consciousness'. The ultimate aim is to write quickly and almost automatically and without undue thought of the shapes of letters, but with the intention of writing well. The fingers should know the shapes of letters, for conscious thought would have to be very fast to control every movement. That is, the aim should be to attend to the end and not the means. Those adults, however, who adopt the italic hand either because they are teachers or because they seek pleasure in the act of writing, will attend to the means as well as the end, since they will be acquiring new skills. Some adults will not mind either the brake put upon speed by learning new writing-habits or a loss of freedom, for they will enjoy the compensation of the attractive interest to be found in italic writing. Certain adults have confessed that in reforming their handwriting the initial slowing down of speed caused by the change in style has improved their English, for they have had more time to choose their words; a second compensation.

Freedom and Control

Control does not imply the writing of a laboured hand that smacks of drawing and excessive precision but rather the attitude of mind that shows determination to write clearly and with grace as well as pace. There are those who prefer so much freedom that legibility is inevitably reduced. They argue that expression of personality has value even when it involves some lack of clarity. Against this plea for expression before function is the more logical one that personality cannot fail to be expressed in good writing as well as in bad if less obtrusively.

Every mature writer reconciles his freedom and control and decides, if subconsciously, on each occasion, as pen touches paper, how much discipline is to be coupled with how much freedom. More discipline, perhaps, in addressing an envelope, less in the drafting of a letter not to be seen by a second person. The child at a junior school will use much discipline. The adolescent will write with as much speed as he can muster when taking notes and so often in the scramble he must sacrifice clarity and grace. At this stage, periods of careful practice can offset the effects of urgency and dash, and they may be used for the making of manuscript books, with or without decoration and illustration (*cf.* page 89).

In the italic hand there is the possibility of writing slowly and with great precision in letter formation to gain a most excellent set script or of writing quickly with rhythmical fluency and free grace.

PRINT-SCRIPT

Print-script (sometimes called 'ball and stick') is a simplified version of the Roman letter. It was introduced into schools following a lecture by the late Edward Johnston to L.C.C. teachers in 1913 when, in making suggestions as to an *ideal* course of teaching handwriting, he showed amongst his alphabets one which later was adapted for school use. Johnston regarded print-script as rather formless skeletons of Roman lower-case letters and did not wish it to be thought he was directly responsible for the form of print-script characters. Print-script is held by teachers of infants, who are doubtless appreciative of its simple character, to be of assistance in teaching both reading and writing, since one alphabet serves the two purposes. It has two shortcomings: there is nothing about it that gives a hint of development into a running hand and it has circular instead of elliptical movements (*cf.* p. 82).

PENMANSHIP, PENS, AND PEN-STROKES

Handwriting is a handicraft. Penmanship implies skill in the use of a tool. Consideration must be given then to the characteristics of the pen and how to use this tool in a skilful way.

On trying a new sort of pen, the user, alert to the appearance of evidence of suitability or unfitness, will notice the feeling of ease or restraint transmitted to the hand by the friction of the pen moving over the paper, and also, probably, how thick are the strokes made and how freely the ink runs. But there is another matter that should have primary consideration: how is gradation of thickness of stroke (that is, 'shading') made by the pen? Some pens such as the stylographic, blunted, or ball-pointed pens, produce no variation in the thickness of stroke, and against these pens it may be said that the stroke of uniform thickness robs writing of a crispness and vitality that pleases the eye, and that shading is a quality not to be renounced.

FIG. 4

Shading can be produced by varying pressure of pen on paper, or by changing direction of stroke, according to whether the pen falls in the category of the 'pointed pen' (Fig. 4*a*), or of the pen often called the 'broad' pen (Fig. 4*b*).

(The 'broad' pen is a pen with an edge instead of a point; and as the edge is not necessarily broad, a better description may be the 'edged' pen.)

The pointed pen is flexible so that pressure may be used to cause shading. Pressure, however, cannot be regulated in fast writing; and scratchy strokes and haphazard shading do not make for quiet beauty. The flexible pointed pen is regarded therefore as unsuitable for italic writing, and will be considered further only in relation to the 'pen-direction' appropriate to its use ('pen-direction' refers to the position of the pen in the hand in relation to the body: for example, whether the pen-shaft points towards the shoulder, or away from it: the angle of the pen-shaft to the horizontal plane may be conditioned by the angle of the slope of the desk and other factors, and that sort of 'pen-inclination' is not intended).

The stiff-edged pen (Fig. 4b) if used without pressure or alteration of pen-direction and with the full width of its edge on the paper will make a stroke of equal thickness so long as its course is

not deflected. The thinnest stroke it produces will be at right-angles to the thickest. Gradation from thin to thick or thick to thin will have mathematical regularity (Fig. 5).

FIG. 5

The angle of the pen's edge to the horizontal writing line is the angle of the thinnest line, and may be called the 'pen-angle'.

Edged pens differ considerably, not only in the width of the edge, but also in the angle of the pen's edge to the slit (Fig. 6).

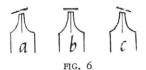

FIG. 6

Looking down on the pens

With a similar pen-direction, but using pens with pen-edges of the three sorts shown in Fig. 6, it would be found that the thinnest or the thickest lines (at right-angles to each other) made naturally by the pen would run in different directions (Fig. 7).

Conversely, if the direction of the thinnest or the thickest strokes

(Note that the arrows run ni the same direction)

FIG. 7

was made the same by each of the three sorts of pen, the pen-direction would vary (Fig. 8).

(Note that the arrows run in different directions)

FIG. 8

Pen-direction must be adjusted correctly to the appropriate pen. This adjustment is considered to be effected by the use of a pen 'square-edged', or as some pen manufacturers curiously describe it 'square-pointed', as in Fig. 4*b*, held so that the pen-shaft is pointed away from the right shoulder in the direction of the right forearm (but ascending), whilst the elbow is held lightly and naturally away from the side of the body. A more precise demonstration of the pen-direction is to hold the pen so, with its edge at about 45° to the writing line of the paper (Figs. 7*b* and 8*b*). The paper should be squarely placed before the demonstrator but slightly to the right of the centre of the body, and the writing lines should be parallel with the edge of the desk. If a child, seated at his desk but without a pen in hand, placed the fingers of the right hand naturally and easily upon the fingers of the left hand, the left hand being upon the desk and the palms prone, the right forearm would probably be found to be in the direction to give the pen-angle (*cf.* Plate 1).

A pen-angle of 45° disposes of thicks and thins in a most convenient way; i.e. it gives sufficient breadth to a letter without producing a sprawling hand, and the horizontal strokes and downstrokes have about equal thickness. In the italic hand, the thickest stroke naturally produced by a pen (see Fig. 5) is not much in evidence. The importance of the pen-angle being not less than 45° is stressed. A check on whether one is writing with a pen-angle of 45° is to make a cross so: ╋. The vertical and the horizontal strokes should be equally thick.

HYGIENE

Such a pen-direction as that advised, and the symmetrical and balanced posture that should go with it, will make for ease and health. There will be no strong invitation to the child when writing to curve his spine sideways, or turn his body, or bend his head over, as he would be likely to do if his pen pointed to his shoulder.

Every attention should be given to posture so that it is natural, healthy, confident, comely, and comfortable. The child should sit erect, with level shoulders parallel to the desk. His feet should be placed firmly in front of him on the floor or foot-rest. Both forearms should rest lightly on the desk to within a short distance of the elbows, one forearm being balanced by the other. The chest should not press against the desk. The body should not be curved nor turned, nor the head bent over sideways, nor inclined unduly forward.

When in individual cases it is necessary to have more support by placing both elbows on the desk, the forearms must still be in balanced positions. If the right elbow is held too far from the body, as by placing it well on the desk, the pen-angle will be greater than 45° and there may be a tendency to write with a backward slope. Some correction would be given by the use of a pen as shown in Fig. 6c, but if such an oblique-edged pen is used, the pen-shaft should still be pointed in the direction of the right forearm.

Undue bending forward may cause eyestrain, shallow breathing, poor circulation, indigestion, and fatigue. A child can bend over a sloped desk less than a flat one, and therefore a slope, if only slight, is desirable on the grounds of health. The professional calligrapher works at a slope of say 45°, sitting up comfortably and seeing his work truly. The steep slope allows the direction of his sight to be at right angles to the writing-surface without his bending forward. To recommend the steep slope for school-children, however, is counsel of perfection, for there are difficulties arising from expense, convenience, and the conditions under which school- and home-work is done. Accordingly it is necessary to consider the child as seated at a flat desk.

The practice of slanting the paper may be good for writing very sloped hands, but it is not required for the models and the posture taught in this book. In order to preserve the pen angle of 45° to the writing line, either the elbow would be forced further from the body, or a different pen would be necessary, namely a pen having an oblique edge (Fig. 6a).

The writer has been advised by an ophthalmic surgeon of his acquaintance that a child's eyes should be from 12 to 14 inches from the writing, for although a child of 8 with normal eyes can see to read or write without strain at 6 inches, the accommodating power of his eyes diminishes as he grows older, and then close reading is a strain. In any case he needs to keep some of this power in reserve. For these reasons alone the child should not be allowed to acquire a habit of close application, or, if a habit has been established, attempts should be made to remedy it. A child's sight will be protected further if he is not required to read or write in a half-light, nor for longer than 25 minutes on end, if always he is placed with the light coming over his left shoulder so that the shadow of the pen is avoided, and if he writes on unglazed paper.

Avoidance of strain will be helped also if one eye is not nearer to the writing than the other and if the writing is not foreshortened. That is to say the child's eye as nearly as possible should be level, and parallel to the writing line, with the direction of his sight at right-angles to the word being written.

Hygiene

The left hand of the child should hold the sheet or exercise book in position and raise the paper when each line is completed. If, where lines are long, the paper is moved to the left at least once after each line is begun, the poise of the head will be less disturbed. Exercise books are usually 8 by 6½ inches. For writing the compressed hands of this book quite half an inch could be spared from the width of the book, or wide side margins allowed, and the shorter line left for writing will tend to take the right hand less far from the centre of the body. As the writing proceeds, the right forearm, which is oblique in relation to the body and to the edge of the desk, should travel a parallel course: that is, it should maintain continuously the same angle to body and desk. The right hand should not swing round, with the elbow as pivot: rather the shoulder should be the pivot and the whole forearm move outwards.

PEN-HOLD

Variations in the structure of hands and arms deter from making hard-and-fast rules as to the 'pen-hold' (as distinct from pen-direction). The modern orthodox pen-hold is to have the pen between the thumb and first finger, and to hold it in place by the tip of the thumb at the side of the pen, the tip of the first finger above, and the top of the second finger bent at an angle to the pen-shaft and supporting the pen by its side. The third finger is against the second, and the fourth (little finger) against the third. The four fingers are held together: that is a condition that suggests restriction, since the two fingers which are directing the pen are not free and away from the others, which are giving purchase.

In the writing book of Urban Wyss (Zurich, 1549), two illustrations of good pen-holdings are given, and in one it is clear that the pen is held by two fingers and thumb, but the third and little fingers are bent well in towards the wrist, and the little finger and the side of the hand are upon the desk. Such a pen-hold would allow much freedom of movement of the pen, and has in its favour that it is the hold which was employed by that calligraphic genius, the late Edward Johnston. The other illustration given by Wyss shows the pen held by the thumb and first finger only, no other finger being in actual contact with the pen. The pen lies along the first finger, the second finger is half bent and the third and fourth fingers again doubled in towards the palm (Fig. 9).

FIG. 9

From Libellus valde doctus *by Urban Wyss. Zurich,* 1549

The author's own pen-hold, which is an uncommon one and not put forward as having value to others, is like the orthodox one except that only one finger is in actual contact with the pen.

The pen-hold should be comfortable and unrestrictive, with the first finger not too near nor too far from the pen's edge. Perhaps the most valuable advice on the pen-hold is negative: the first

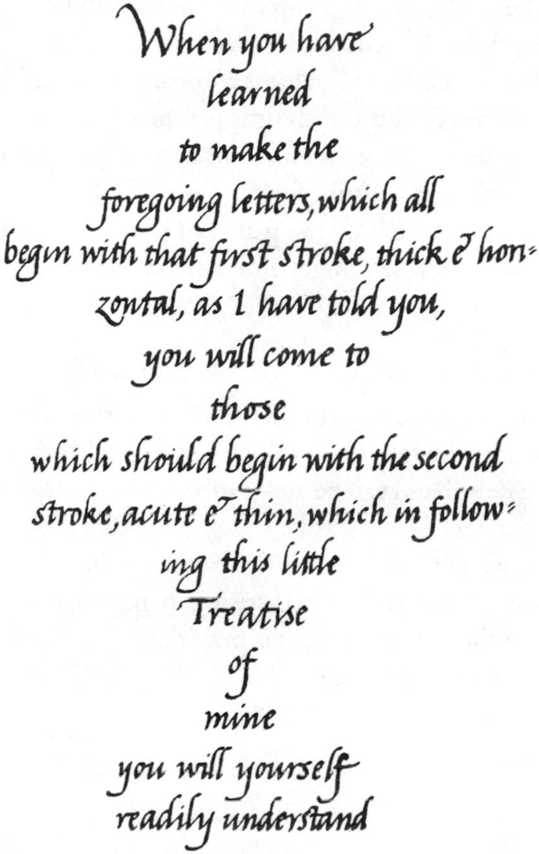

When you have
learned
to make the
foregoing letters, which all
begin with that first stroke, thick & horizontal, as 1 have told you,
you will come to
those
which should begin with the second
stroke, acute & thin, which in following this little
Treatise
of
mine
you will yourself
readily understand

FIG. 10

*A page of Arrighi's manual translated by Miss Anna Hornby and written
by her with her left hand*

finger certainly should not be bent at right angles, but this statement must be qualified by saying that the fault must be expected in the young child. A mediaeval scribe wrote: '*Three fingers write, and the whole body is in travail*'. That is true particularly of the young child, often writing with tightly gripped pen and, perhaps, with protruding tongue. The pen should not lie low in the hollow between first finger and thumb, for the flow of ink will be lessened by the lowered elevation of the pen, and this grasp and position also tends to increase finger-movements and lessen hand-movements.

LEFT-HANDED WRITERS

A happy circumstance for the left-handed is that although our written alphabets have been developed by right-handed penmen, the italic hand can be and is successfully written by the left-hander. The upstroke rising at about 45° can be made a hairline stroke with little friction if the nib is sharply oblique (Fig. 11). The writing paper may be

FIG. 11

canted so that the left side is higher than the right. The left elbow is kept to the side of the body.

HAND-MOVEMENTS, PRESSURE, AND TOUCH

Holding the pen with the pen-direction already indicated, and raising it a little from the paper, it will be noticed that when the fingers and thumb are contracted, as in making a downstroke, and then extended, in the to-and-fro movements of the pen's edge the pen rises and falls but little. That is, the easy movements of the fingers and thumb give direction to the pen, but they would cause very slight 'writing-pressure' if the pen were in contact with the paper. If, however, the pen-shaft were pointing to the right shoulder, the elbow close to the side and the palm of the hand turned over towards the desk, the bending of the first two fingers and thumb would cause the pen's edge to be elevated or lowered, to be directed and pressed or released. There would be an up-and-down movement, as well as a to-and-fro movement. The pen's edge would approach the paper and recede from it. For this reason the pliable pointed pen generally is rightly taught to be held with the pen-shaft pointing to the shoulder in order to gain shading by pressure from the bending of the fingers, as in Civil Service or copperplate hands: a bad posture fit for the use of a bad pen.

Sometimes the edged pen is too flexible; and also is employed with the pen-direction appropriate to writing with pressure.

The italic script depends upon the pen producing the thicks, thins, and gradations.

Whilst the square-edged pen should be used without a consciously controlled regulation of pressure to effect gradation of stroke (shading), generally there will be some degree of pressure of the pen on paper (writing-pressure). Fatigue is reduced by rhythmical alternation of contraction and relaxation of muscles. Close the hand tightly and it soon tires, but continually open and close it and very much less fatigue is felt. So it is expected in the case of the older child and the mature penman that in holding the square-edged pen with the pen direction away from the shoulder there will be but slight rhythmical alternation of writing-pressure and relaxation, and much greater pressure elsewhere, either of two fingers and thumb ('grip-pressure') or of little finger and/or of wrist on paper. The late Edward Johnston barely gripped the pen: his grip was so light, as a rule, that it was perfectly easy to slide the shaft in and out of the triangle of fingers and thumb. He considered this light grip enabled him to feel to some degree whether the nib's edge was in true contact with the writing-surface. Edward Johnston, however, pressed his hand firmly upon the desk. The grip-pressure of the orthodox holding would not be so light.

The young child writing with considerable grip-pressure will doubtless also write with corresponding heavy writing-pressure.

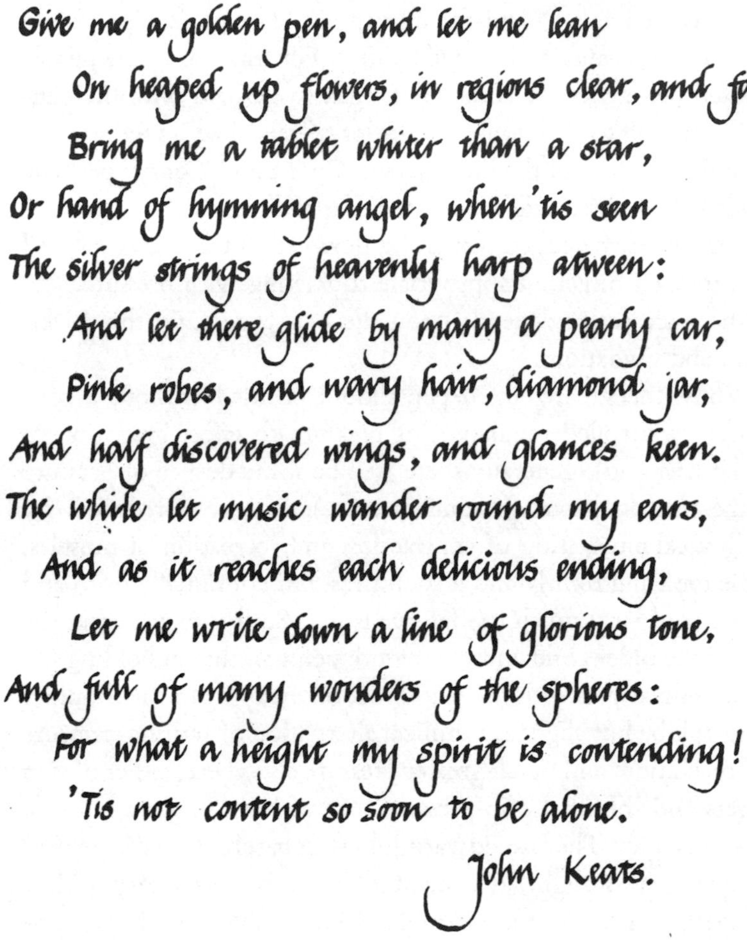

Give me a golden pen, and let me lean
   On heaped up flowers, in regions clear, and far;
   Bring me a tablet whiter than a star,
Or hand of hymning angel, when 'tis seen
The silver strings of heavenly harp atween:
   And let there glide by many a pearly car,
   Pink robes, and wavy hair, diamond jar;
And half discovered wings, and glances keen.
The while let music wander round my ears,
   And as it reaches each delicious ending,
   Let me write down a line of glorious tone,
And full of many wonders of the spheres:
   For what a height my spirit is contending!
   'Tis not content so soon to be alone.

                    John Keats.

FIG. 12
Writing by Anne Giddings. Aged 14. Devizes Grammar School

Lawn as white as driven snow;
Cyprus black as e'er was crow;
Gloves as sweet as damask roses;
Masks for faces and for noses;
Bugle bracelets, necklace amber,
Perfume for a lady's chamber;
Golden quoifs and stomachers,
For my lads to give their dears:
Pins and poking-sticks of steel,
What maids lack from head to heel:
Come buy of me, come; come buy, come buy;
Buy, lads, or else your lasses cry:
Come buy.

FIG. 13
Writing by John Howells. Aged 14. Devizes Grammar School

Writing-pressure was stated by the late Robert Saudek, a scientific graphologist, to be 'so absolutely bound up with, and typical of, the personality of the writer that far-reaching psychological conclusions could be drawn from it'. The only case he had come across, 'out of tens of thousands, where two persons had the same writing-pressure was that of a pair of identical conjoint twins who lived on the same blood stream'. In the face of such a statement the only advice about touch that can be offered is that it is desirable it should be light. Some of the movements of writing involve pushing the pen against its edge, and though a turning movement immediately reduces the resistance, a light touch will also ease the motion.

RECOMMENDED PENS

Pens fall roughly into three categories:

(a) those that are pointed and make thicks and thins and gradations by pressure and release of pressure,

(b) those that have an edge and make thicks, thins and gradations by a change in direction of the movement of the stroke rather than by pressure, and

(c) those that write much as a pencil does, without thicks, thins, and gradations.

The italic hands of the fifteenth and sixteenth centuries were written with quills that normally fall in category (b), but sometimes with blunt pens making little contrast between thicks and thins (category (c)). The blunt quills may have been worn but possibly on occasion were cut so as to be blunt and more easy-running, for sharply cut quills tend to kick and splutter when pushed against the edge. The pens of category (a) are appropriate to copperplate or to copperplate-derivatives and are not recommended. The pen that is recommended is that of category (*b*).

Another division is into categories of dip-pens and fountain-pens.

The first dip-pens for italic writing were made at my suggestion by the pen firm, Geo. W. Hughes, namely the *Flight Commander* pen, but they are no longer available. These were easy-running metal alloy stubs with a straight edge. Most stubs have either a blunt point or an oblique edge, but there are straight-edged nibs made in an *Italic* series in five breadths, with a companion set for left-handers, namely by William Mitchell (British Pens Ltd., Bearwood Road, Smethwick, Birmingham).

The steel 'J' pen is too flexible for most people. One needs to be very light-fingered if the points are not to spread. On the other hand, a pen with very little flexibility, such as a manifold-ing nib, can be tiring to use.

Some nibs may be fitted with a reservoir (e.g. William Mitchell's *Slippon Reservoir*) or to a pen-holder fitted with a reservoir (e.g. William Mitchell's Reservoir Holder, or Dryad P.20 penholder). The Osmiroid *Italic 95* nibs have a satisfactory built-in reservoir.

The full width of the edge of the pen must be in contact with the paper when writing. Because it makes a marked contrast of thick and thin strokes it will impose a certain discipline on the hand, which may be good for a learner old enough to cope with an italic pen. For left-handers the writing-edge will be angled to the left.

Hand-processes are involved in the making of gold fountain-pen nibs and consequently no two are quite alike. The Parker Pen Co. offer a choice of italic nibs with their Parker 45 and 65 ranges. There are inexpensive fountain pens with interchangeable italic nibs in different widths which are liked by adults as well as by children. Such pens are *Platignum* (Mentmore Manufac-turing Co., Stevenage) and *Osmiroid* (E. S. Perry, Gosport).

FIG. 14

From Opera nella quale si insegna a scrivere *by Augustino da Siena.*
Venice, 1568

PENHOLDERS

The author is not aware of any research made as to the most suitable sizes and types of penholders. A warning seems desirable that considerable fatigue may be caused if the barrel of the pen is too large or too small in diameter or if the pen is too heavy or too light, but being closely connected with touch it is largely a personal matter and comfort is the significant virtue. The author's favourite wooden penholder is 7½ inches long and tapers 3 inches from the thicker end. Such a length, of course, is not essential for comfort, but this pen has good balance.

PENCILS, FELT PENS AND CHALKS

For infants, thick pencils such as *Black Beauty* and *Black Prince* are recommended. Carpenter's pencils, which do make thicks and thins, are not easy to use satisfactorily and tend to encourage writing with pressure. Moreover, the lead quickly needs re-sharpening.

The practice of writing with felt pens on old newspapers turned through 90° offends the author's sense of fitness.

Naturally, it is desirable for the teacher to acquire a good technique of writing with chalk on blackboard. When demonstrating in the handwriting lesson the teacher can write with thicks and thins by cutting slices off the point of his chalk (back and front) to make a wedge. Also he may break his chalk and write with a fragment held between thumb and forefinger, the outer surface making contact with the board. At other times he may well feel that provided he makes good shapes he can use his chalk as he would a pencil, and that the pupil's edged pens will give them the linear quality. There is a chalk with a rectangular section, namely *Bedford de Luxe* Lettering Chalk (Cosmic Crayon Co. Ltd.).

PAPER

Francis Clement in 'The Petie Schole' (A.D. 1587) says the 'whitest, finest, and smoothest paper is best'. Undoubtedly this is still true. A smooth paper reduces friction and resistance to the pen and gives a sharpness to writing. The paper should not be glossy, however. Many italic writers use Spicer's Calligrapher's Paper and Dickenson's Three Candlesticks but there are numerous suitable writing papers besides.

INK

No special ink is required for italic handwriting. For those who like a permanent black ink there are Waterman's *Midnight Black*, Waterman's Calligraph Ink, Stephen's Calligraphic Ink, and *Quink Permanent Black* and also various carbon inks, which are made for both dip-pens and fountain-pens. Higgins Eternal Ink is American and unfortunately difficult to obtain in England.

If a carbon ink is used in a fountain-pen it needs frequent cleaning.

ECONOMY OF STROKES AND EFFORT

The letters of the formal Roman hand are built up by fitting stroke to stroke, the pen being frequently lifted. The strokes are principally downward strokes made by the pen being pulled by the contraction of fingers and thumb. Thus an 'm' is made of three main pulled strokes fitted together (Fig. 2*a*), with perhaps other strokes added for beauty's sake or for other reasons. Speed will simplify the method of construction, as already explained, so that the letter is made with one continuous stroke (Fig. 2*b*), or, if other letters are joined to it, by the part of one continuous deflecting stroke (Fig. 20).

In the transition from formal to cursive, speed introduced the upstroke, and in so doing reduced the number of strokes used for the formation of letters, tied some letters together, narrowed the letters, and constrained the ample arch. The assistance to speed given by the upstroke will depend upon the suitability of the adjustment of the pen to the paper, for most edged pens are inclined to resist, and perhaps to splutter, if pushed against the pen's edge. The maximum resistance offered by paper to pen (excluding degrees of pressure from consideration) is when the pen is pushed away from the writer in the direction which produces the thickest stroke. No resistance troubles and impedes the pen if the upstroke is 'sidled': that is, if the pen is moved sideways so that the thinnest stroke marks the paper.

A carefully cut chisel-edged quill pen gives the greatest resistance to the pushed stroke, and also allows the making of the thinnest of sideways strokes. In contrast to the quill among edged pens is the fountain pen. The resistance of paper to pen will be affected by the smoothness or otherwise of the surface of the paper, as well as by the character of the pen and the pressure used. Whether, however, fountain pen or a sharper pen, or smooth or rough paper, or pressure or little pressure, are used, most fluent writers do sidle upstrokes; but because the direction of the pen is frequently towards the shoulder, or the pen-hold is appropriate to that pen-direction, letters tend to be flattened and widely spaced in the construction of words (Fig. 15).

FIG. 15

Fast writing is made up of pulled, sidled, and pushed strokes; but where the pushed stroke occurs the tendency of the fluent pen is strong to avoid resistance, as, for example, by turning the pushed stroke quickly into another and easier direction (note the top of the bow of the letter *a*).

MOVEMENT AND JOINS

The pen is moved and lays a trail of ink. In the italic hand the trail is not the whole record of the movements made by the pen's a ex c &ı hoc ordine c ꝑ a ꝗ .

b ex l &ı ſic l l b , vel b
ex l ꝛ & ı ſic , l l l b , ſed
priore modo certius .

c initio huius capitis figurata eſ ꞇ .

d ex c clauſo ſic ꝺ & l hoc ordine
ꝺ ꝺ ꝺ d , ab ꝺ autē in ſequentis
elementi caput transferendus
eſ ꞇ calamus tenuiſſimi ductus
via , ſic ꝺ ꝺ ꝺ d , quo certior
fiat per huius ꝺ roſtrū
deſcenſus .

e ex ı ſed paululum inuariato ,
tenuiſſima enim linea non à
perpendiculari debet egredi , ſed
à breuiſſima latiſſimi ductus par
ticula tali . ꝰ , quę mediocri –

point, for contact is frequently lost, the pen often rising from the paper in very small jumps from one letter to another as well as from word to word. A set italic hand can be written with too many jumps for speed, such as, for example, where the letter *m* is made with two pen-lifts. A fast writer will probably find himself writing several letters without a pen-lift, whilst in contrast some young child may tend to write the letter *n* with an interior pen-lift. The pen-lifts are means of avoiding awkward joins, and they also offer opportunities for adjusting the hand as it passes from left to right across the paper, and these brief interruptions of touch actually afford relaxation in the effort of writing. The copperplate models require all letters to be joined, but to the author it seems more desirable to break the continuity as convenient. If it were essential to join all letters then some of the letters of the italic alphabet would need to be redesigned.

Joins are undoubtedly agents of speed. Indeed the diagonal join, which is such a common, significant, and dominant feature in Mercator's example (Fig. 16), tends to govern the shape of many letters and should receive due consideration in the design of a model. For example, in the letter *a* there are two strokes that rise. The second upstroke, which completes the letter, will frequently run on into the next letter: i.e. will become a diagonal join. For this reason, the first upstroke of the *a* should have relationship to the second, which may become the join, so that one is not required to make two quite differently shaped upstrokes. Thus economy and unity serve speed.

The diagonal join is found in most words of the completed model. The other join commonly required is the horizontal join.

The principal movements in the model alphabet of italic minuscules of this book are in making:

Straight downstrokes |||| *hill*

Upstrokes and diagonal joins	//// *nun*
Horizontal strokes and joins	--- *ton*
Clockwise curves	*mmm* *bhkmnpr*
Counter-clockwise curves	*uuuu* *acdeglqtu*
Ellipses	*oooo*
Angles	*wwww* *vow*
Pushed strokes	*≂ adf ⟨ fgjs*
Serifs	*ι inu*

In Arrighi's manual the first instruction is in making two strokes: one is thick and horizontal (cf. Fig. 10).

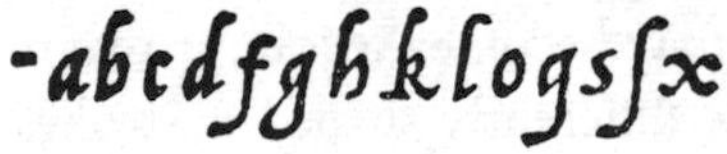

-abcdfghklogsſx

FIG. 17

(A surprising fact is that Arrighi's thick horizontal stroke, equivalent to Palatino's *testa*, is made by a return movement, from left to right and then, retracing its path, from right to left. Except, for example, when a diagonal join precedes (say) *a, c, d, g, q*, this double movement seems unnecessary today because we have easy-running pens and smooth paper, and so do not have to avoid

46

a pen spluttering, as a quill used in writing on a rough surface may do.)

The other, thin and acute

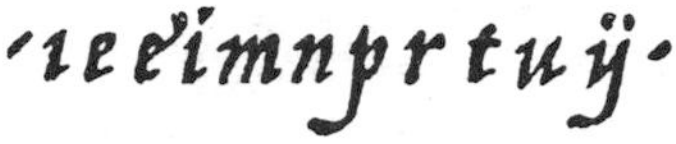

FIG. 18

This movement is appropriate to *e* and *t* when it is a preceding diagonal join.

Palatino, in his manual published 22 years later (Fig. 19), stresses three movements in the alphabet: *testa, traverso,* and *taglio. Testa* refers to the to-and-fro horizontal stroke at the head of *a* and *f, traverso* to the downstroke, and *taglio* to the thin upstroke. Palatino's *testa* is thicker than his *traverso.* His *taglio* rises at about the same angle as the hair-line of the models of this book. His script, however, is narrow and compacted, hardly giving room for the pen to turn round, and tends to a gothic angularity. It is not recommended as a model except as regards unity of style and spacing.

In fast writing, downstrokes intended to be quite straight tend to take on some slight curvature.

FAMILY CHARACTERISTICS OF LETTERS

A good alphabet can be compared to a large family where family-likeness can be seen in the members to a greater or lesser degree. Of the near affinities, *n* is close to *u* and *m, u* to *a, a* to *d, i* to *j, v* to *w,* etc. The family relationships and homogeneity give harmony and readableness to the script. A letter, however, must be sufficiently unlike all other letters as to be recognized with ease and certainty if it is not to fail of its purpose, so that an *n* will not be read for a *u,* a *b* for an *h,* or an *h* for a *k,* etc. So long as letters

47

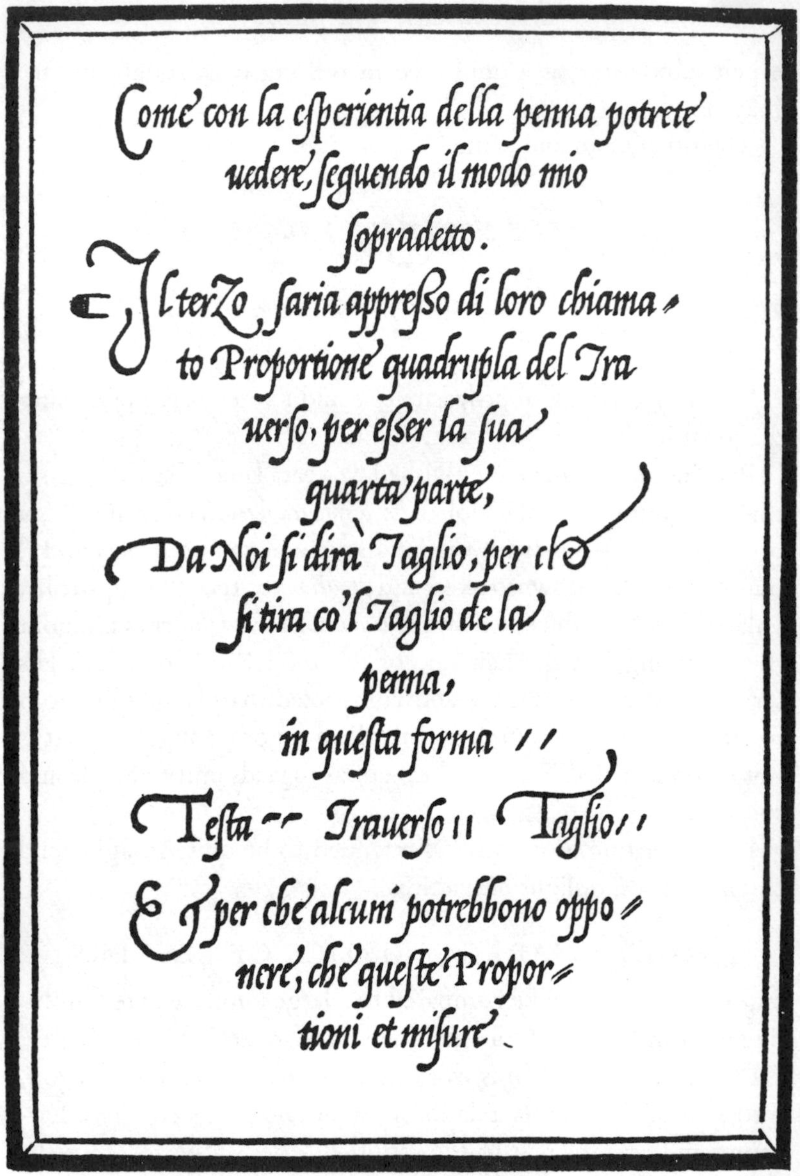

Come con la esperientia della penna potrete
uedere, seguendo il modo mio
sopradetto.
Il terzo, saria appresso di loro chiama-
to Proportione quadrupla del Tra
uerso, per esser la sua
quarta parte,
Da Noi si dirà Taglio, per c'
si tira co'l Taglio de la
penna,
in questa forma //

Testa -- Trauerso || Taglio //

E per che alcuni potrebbono oppo-
nere, che queste Propor-
tioni et misure

FIG. 19

From Libro nel qual s'insegna *by* G. B. Palatino. Rome, 1544
In the author's possession

are distinctive, the closer the relationship in form that the letters of an alphabet have to each other, the greater the possibility of legibility, speed, and beauty. In a sense, each letter has the right to be considered important for legibility and beauty, but it must take a disciplined part in the construction of words.

The author recommends that the alphabet should be learnt by grouping the letters as in Fig. 22.

CLOCKWISE AND COUNTER-CLOCKWISE MOVEMENTS

Good writing is rhythmical and patterned. In designing a cursive hand the calligrapher should consider the basic rhythms (or patterns) to be used in the model so that his slowly written models are simple and suitable for fast legible writing. This implies he must take particular care in designing the *n* and the *u* (see Fig. 20).

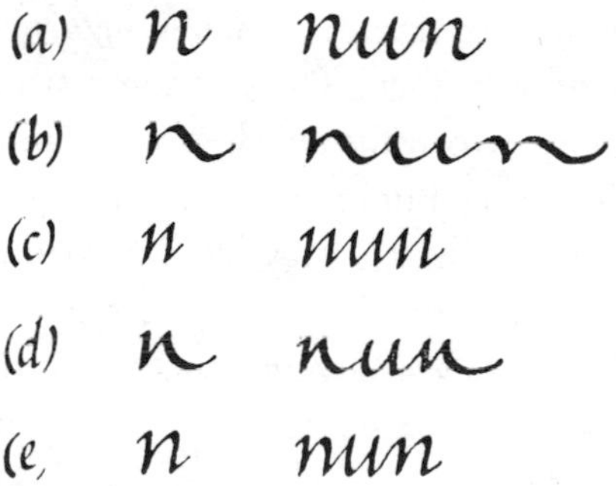

(a) *n   nun*

(b) *n   nun*

(c) *n   nun*

(d) *n   nun*

(e, *n   nun*

FIG. 20

The *n* is roughly an inversion of the *u* (it is hardly likely to be exactly the same shape), the *n* having an arch and the *u* an inverted arch. There is, however, an important difference in the letters caused by the inversion: the *n* includes an up-and-over, or clockwise, movement and the *u* an under-and-up, or counter-clockwise, movement (these clockwise and counter-clockwise movements are not circular in character, but nearly elliptical).

This distinction divides up a considerable part of the alphabet into groups of related letters. Those letters in the models of this book with a more or less dominant clockwise movement are *b*, *h*, *k*, *m*, *n*, *p*, and *r*, those with a more or less dominant counter-clockwise movement are *a*, *c*, *d*, *e*, *g*, *o*, *q*, *t*, and *u* (but *e*, when made of two strokes, and *g* have both movements and so too have *f* and *s*).

For fast writing it would be easier if all or most of the letters of the alphabet were to be written with a counter-clockwise rhythm, but we have inherited an alphabet that cannot be adapted to this pattern without a reduction of the standard of legibility. The calligrapher's problem is therefore to design a hand which, when written quickly, allows the possibility of reconciling the contrary rhythms, and therefore of *n* and *u* made with sufficient difference to ensure that an *n* does not look like a *u*.

It may be argued that if the *n* is commonly written as a *u*, the eye will perceive the correct intention and '*auuouuce*' will be read as '*announce*'. So why bother? There is some truth in this argument, for in reading a word the eye does not depend always upon recognizing all the letters, but may identify the word by its general appearance. A group of letters may be identified as a word even when certain letters are missing: e.g., ph t gr ph. However, a model is offered that may allow and encourage the writing of *n* and *u* with sufficient distinctiveness, as an alternative to accepting the probability of debasement. The reader at this stage is invited to study the *n*'s and *u*'s of Plates 4, 5, 7, 10 and 16.

SIMPLE RHYTHMS AND ANGULARITY

Doubtless there are still many children (other than those writing print-script) who are required to make pot-hooks and hangers, as for example in writing copperplate, business, or Civil Service hands. But a fast writer will be a rare exception who can retain both the curves of the arch and the inverted arch terminating *n* (as shown in Fig. 20*a*) without a breakdown of one or other. The contrary swing of such curves (clockwise and counter-clockwise) is against speed. The common failure shows itself by the introduction of angularity or by a more undulating curve due to the stressing of the counter-clockwise movements. Most rhythms which arise from the way the letters *n* and *u* and their kindred letters are made can be related to, or recognized as, one or other of those roughly indicated in Fig. 20, although occasionally two of these rhythms will appear in the same adult's handwriting.

These are simple rhythms; and they are intermittent, since certain letters of the alphabet do not conform to them. They become more powerful in fast writing when letters are tied together by diagonal joins (as *n* would be tied to *u*), for the diagonal joins not only conform to the rhythm but frequently carry it on from letter to letter. (There is also a more complicated rhythm in a piece of fluent and developed handwriting which is an expression of the skill, mental and physical characteristics, and style of the penman, and is outside the sphere of this manual.)

If both the arch of the *n* and the inverted arch of the end of this letter which turns and extends to make the join (i.e., both the curves) as in Fig. 20*a* could be preserved, then the rhythm of Fig. 20*a* would have a claim for acceptance in an exemplar hand. As already shown, however, this rhythm will not stand the stress of speed. The introduction into a model of a feature not essential for legibility and of such importance in structure and rhythm seems ill-advised if there is not some fitness for the purpose of speed.

There may be a tendency to angularity then, either in the tops or bottoms of letters, or in both, or an undulating spread pattern as in Fig. 15. The latter is unlikely to be pleasant. Because downstrokes may be strongly pulled counter-clockwise by the flexing of fingers and thumb, the rhythm is commonly as at *d*, Fig. 20. For legibility, it would be better to have curves than angles at the tops of letters, as in rhythm *e*, for the eyes, in the rapid movements they make in reading, take little account of the bottoms of letters (see Fig. 3, which shows how little the bottoms of letters may assist identification). This argument is one that has even greater significance in the design of type, where the standard of legibility is very high.

If the recommendation in this manual were to direct the pen to the right shoulder, instead of to the elbow, rhythm *e* would be too difficult, but with the pen-direction as already advised and described, this difficulty seems to the author to be removed. With the pen inclined to the right shoulder, the easiest movement in writing is one made of contracting fingers and thumb and is a downward pulled stroke. The pulled stroke is then much stronger than the upstroke made by extending the fingers and thumb. But if the pen-direction is away from the shoulder and the pen is as suggested in this book, then the sideways movement of the hand produces a sidled upstroke with about as much ease as it makes a pulled downstroke. The sideways movement of the hand if the pen-direction is towards the shoulder is almost horizontal, and accordingly the writing is flattened (Fig. 15). If the pen-direction is away from the shoulder, the sideways movement of the hand is more oblique (Fig. 14), and so letters may have a more suitable height, an upstanding sturdiness, and be more closely spaced.

Rhythm *c*, Fig. 20, makes for slowness (as may be demonstrated easily by the experiment of making a number of zig-zags, and rounded arches, and inverted arches, and comparing the times taken) and for this reason to a breakdown into curvature, probably counter-clockwise. Also it confuses and unifies *n* and *u*.

Rhythm *e*, as exemplified in Fig. 20, has some angularity at the bottoms of letters, particularly at the terminals of *a*, *d*, *h*, *i*, *m*, *n*, and *u*, when the terminals are extended to make diagonal joins. The rhythm was chosen for the exemplar hand of this manual as being the best of the simple rhythms and one which reconciles the clockwise and counter-clockwise movements of *n* and *u*. Had rhythm *d* been selected, *n* would have tended to assume the shape of *u*.

It is to be explained that sharp angles, as in the bottoms of letters of the script in Fig. 38, when writing with pace are likely to become naturally and pleasingly something nearer to very narrow curves, and Plates 4 and 7 are of interest in this connection.

COMPRESSION OF LETTERS

The extent to which the arches of *h*, *m*, *n*, etc., are curved need not be the subject of a rule, but in a mature hand where conscious design and discipline break down to some degree through speed, and the upward sidled stroke ascends at an angle of at least 45°, there is not likely to be that roundness and broadness of form to be seen in the Roman letters and which may be given in print-script letters by the young child drawing (rather than writing) them in a careful way—and teachers must resign themselves to the loss of a feature they may like. But the narrower letter of the sixteenth-century has its own elegance and grace. The fifteenth-century italic letter was often a less compressed letter than that of Arrighi, for it had not broken free from the influence of the Caroline script—a script not cursive though having some cursive characteristics in the ninth century.

SLANT OF WRITING

The slope of letters in the models is slightly to the right, but the italic hand can be written with upright strokes or even with a slant to the left, though the latter is generally considered to be a displeasing characteristic. It seems a proper thing for writing to reflect the trend from left to right by a forward slope. Italic types used by contemporary printers generally slant 12° or more from the vertical. Italics are used by the printer principally for contrast and the marked slope is a means of distinction. In writing this does

not apply. The slope of models in the earliest writing books ranges
from 5° to 10°.

The downstroke which has a slight forward slant is not the
easiest stroke to make. If one bends fingers and thumbs in towards
the palm quite naturally, the pen, if held as recommended, is
moved in this direction: ↘ (that is, towards the elbow). A backhand may therefore be due to too great an economy or avoidance
of effort, and then it should be corrected by drills or other in-
centives to a more disciplined action. A backhand may also be due
to the right elbow being too far from the body, to too strong a
use of the thumb, or not enough movement of the hand, or to
fashion among children. According to graphologists, there may
also be psychological reasons (*cf.* page 38).

*abcdefghijklmn
opqrstuvwxyyz*

FIG. 21

THE MINUSCULE ALPHABET

When learning a new hand the pupil must write slowly and with
control of the pen so that the letters he makes are as near as possible to those of the model. That is, the pupil must become completely familiar with the forms of the letters by looking at them
and by writing them. In a sense, the fingers as well as the eyes must
get to know the letters. For this reason it may be helpful to trace
the letters of a model with a dry pen to learn the necessary movements which make the letter-shapes. Jean de Beauchesne wrote:
'*To folowe strang hand with drie penne first prove*', and so this advice
is not new.

ilt adgqu ceo nmr bhk vwy fs jp xz

ilt ilt ilt ilt ilt

adgqu adgqu adgqu adgqu adgqu

ceo ceo ceo ceo ceo

nmr nmr nmr nmr nmr nmr

bhk bhk bhk bhk

nmrbhk nmrbhk nmrbhk nmrbhk

vwy vwy vwy

fs fs fs fs fs fs   sf sf sf sf sf sf

jp jp jp jp jp jp jp

xz xz xz xz

abcdefghijklmnopqrstuvwxyz adgqu

FIG. 22

From Beacon Writing Book Five (*Ginn and Co. Ltd*)

It is important to remember when practising that italic letters are not circular and are not widely spread. The letters are a little narrow and are placed somewhat closely together in making words.

As handwriting is a system of movements it is convenient to group letters as in Fig. 22.

The letters *i*, *l*, *t* should slope to the right but only slightly. The downstroke turns in a narrow bend and terminates when it becomes a hairline: i.e. when rising at about 45°.

The next family of letters begins with *a*. This letter is not merely a line swung round and up in a somewhat elliptical fashion to be continued in a downstroke: it is made of strokes that vary in thickness as they bend and which enclose a space ('counter') that may be subtle and delightful in shape. The enclosed shape cannot be formed precisely, as if drawn, when writing quickly, and yet a good penman will know and see that letters are made of both strokes and spaces. Fig. 23 gives a rough idea of the shape that attracts the author.

FIG. 23

The letter begins with an almost horizontal stroke (Palatino's *testa*) by pushing the pen against its edge and turning the direction of the stroke sharply downwards: Thus the stroke, fairly thick at first, thins and softly thickens as it descends: (At the base it bends sharply in a narrow curve (almost an angle) to rise in a hair-line to meet the beginning of the letter: *0* The up-stroke should join up with the beginning of the letter and leave no breach. The softly-gradating flatly-curving downstroke is in sympathy with the slope of the writing. That is, the two down-strokes are as nearly parallel as a curve can be to a straight line.

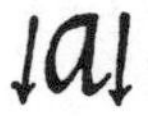

ial The rising hair-line is in accord with the diagonal joins of the script made by the pen in a sideways movement. The second downstroke, quite straight in the model, when written fluently may perhaps tend to the merest suggestion of a curve under the influence of rhythm and of the first, slightly bowed, downstroke. Again there is a sharp bend to the hair-line, in accord now with the character of the first upward bend, and the stroke may end as soon as it becomes a hair-line or it may rise to form a diagonal join: *aan*

In this one letter there is a pushed stroke, two different (but somewhat parallel) downstrokes, and two different upstrokes; and yet all are related and unified by the pen and the rhythm of the hand. The unity contributes to economy. For speed, it is desirable to restrict not only the number of movements but also the kind of movements. Much of the rhythm is implicit in the narrow bend of the stroke to form the hair-line, for the rhythm of the writing grows naturally out of the alphabet. It is also to be remarked that the incidence of the thicker strokes at the upper part of the letter is an aid to legibility, whilst the upstroke, being a hairline, facilitates speed.

The proportions of *a* will set a standard to which all other letters should conform as much as can be arranged. What the proportions shall be is a matter of taste, but the pen itself and the way it is held have some control. Obviously if an *a* is narrow, an *n* or an *o* should not be wide, or vice versa. The letters *a*, *b*, *d*, *g*, *h*, *n*, *o*, *p*, *q* and *u* should have equal width of body.

Much of the above will be seen without indication and appreciated immediately by adult and child. It is as well, however, to bear in mind that though letters are entities they are subordinate to the rhythm of the hand and they may and should contribute to the flowing pattern.

A sketch in Arrighi's manual is the following which may be helpful to those used to making circular movements. But this is but a hint and not a preparatory drill or exercise.

∧∧∧∧∧∧∧∧∧∧∧∧

nunununununununununununun

mamamamamamamamamam

vuvuvuvuvuvu wnwnwnwnw

ancndnengnonqn buhukumunur

mambmcmdmemfmgmhmimjm

kmlmmmnmompmqmrmsmtm

umvmwmxmymzm

abcdefghijklmnopqrstuvwxyz

d, e, f, p, t, x, are made of two strokes:

cld ee ſf pp lt ∖x

1234567890   1234567890

FIG. 24
Dryad Writing Card No. 1 (Dryad Press, Leicester)

Following the significant letter *a*, it is appropriate to practise next the related letters *d*, *g*, *q*, and *u*. The letter *d*, if made with one continuous stroke, would require the pen to rise from the bottom bend to (say) twice the height of *a*. For this reason it will be easier to have a pen-lift when learning the letter. Another factor is that even some young children like to begin the second downstroke (following the pen-lift) with something formed and interesting, which requires a pen-lift (see page 64).

The letter *g* begins as does *a*. It has, however, a clockwise movement in its tail. As the pen turns clockwise it will find some resistance in the movement against its edge. The secret of a good tail to a *g* is in a light touch and a light heart. The second downstroke when written freely will probably take on a slight curvature in anticipation of the swing of the tail. Some humanistic cursives show a letter related to the g of Roman type: *g g* These forms, though good because they are both legible and pleasing, require more care and take more time than the *g* of the model. The letter *q*, again beginning like *a*, ends with a formed short stroke, either lozenged or barbed: *q q* In the Renaissance it was often made so: *g*, but this character is too near *g* to be distinctive enough today. Another form is *Q* . The principal movement of the letter *u* is counter-clockwise. It begins with a serif (a quickly turned curving movement of small compass) and ends as the letter *a*. Other important letters with a counter-clockwise accent are *c*, *e*, and *o*. The letter *c* is not circular but should show some relationship to the first downstroke of *a*, which is a flattened curve. The bow of the *e* is formed by a simple swing. The bend at the base of *c* and *e* is less narrow than in *a*. (Another form of *e* is given in Fig. 34.) The *o*, made without a pen-lift, is elliptical in trend, but because the edged pen gives it thicks, thins, and gradations, and the bottom bend tends to be like that of *a*, it is not quite a true ellipse, though it may well be thought of as one.

Another small group of letters has a clockwise accent: *b*, *h*, *k*, *m*, *n*, and *r*. The letter *n* has initial and terminal serifs as in *u*. When the first downstroke ends, the stroke rises up the stem and then branches to make an arch (without a pen-lift) in a manner somewhat suggestive of the flight of a rocket or the spray of a fountain:

That is, it goes up and away from the stem, over in a sharp bend, and drops—though not vertically. The letter *m* is obviously related to *n*. The letter *r* is like an incomplete *n*. The branching from the stem should occur high enough to prevent the letter looking like *v*. The letter *h* is like the *n* except for the ascender. The letter *b* is related to the *h* but the second downstroke turns in

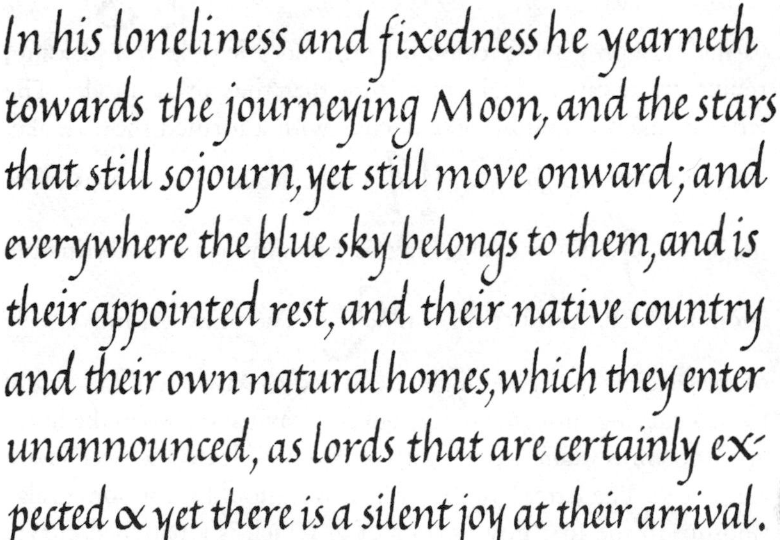

In his loneliness and fixedness he yearneth towards the journeying Moon, and the stars that still sojourn, yet still move onward; and everywhere the blue sky belongs to them, and is their appointed rest, and their native country and their own natural homes, which they enter unannounced, as lords that are certainly expected ∝ yet there is a silent joy at their arrival.

FIG. 25

(*From the gloss of* The Rime of the Ancient Mariner
by Samuel Taylor Coleridge)

horizontally to join the stem. The right hand side of the bow should have the same flatness and tendency to being parallel with the straight downstroke which was noted in the letter *a*. The letter *k* begins as *h* does, but turns into the stem in a curve and springs away obliquely. The bow should be small and should not extend far down the letter. The letter *p* is made of two strokes. It begins with a barbed serif slightly higher than the succeeding bow, which is related to the bow of *b*. The first downstroke ends in a leftward turn with the pen moving lightly against its edge, but it could terminate as does *q*. The bow completes the letter by joining the downstroke horizontally and not at an angle.

The letters *i*, *l*, and *t* terminate much as does *a*. The horizontal stroke of *t* occurs at a height not above that of *a*. The *j* is like an *i* except for the descender, and is related to *p*.

The letters *f* and *s* are related, for each begins with a counter-clockwise movement as well as beginning and ending with pushed strokes. The *s* starts with a small rounded curve and ends with a larger one, but the *f* begins and ends with a tendency to flatness. The middle of the *s* has an oblique direction from top left to bottom right: i.e. not a horizontal stress. In some sixteenth-century writing manuals the ascender of *f* is not so tall as those of *b*, *d*, *h*, *k*, and *l*, and this is regarded as good design.

The remaining letters of the alphabet, *v*, *w*, *x*, *y*, and *z*, are angular in this model. The letters *v* and *w* begin with a serif and end with a restricted movement to the left. The *v* must be quite distinct from the *r*. The letter *y* begins like the *v* and ends with a downstroke turning leftwards, much as does *j* and *f*. A variation is a letter made of two strokes. The three letters *v*, *w*, and *y* should not be wide. The letter *x* is made of two strokes: the first from top left to bottom right and the second either from top right to bottom left or bottom left to top right. The last letter of the alphabet lacks close relationship with other members. The *z*, lending itself to ornamental extension, was often flourished in Italian models,

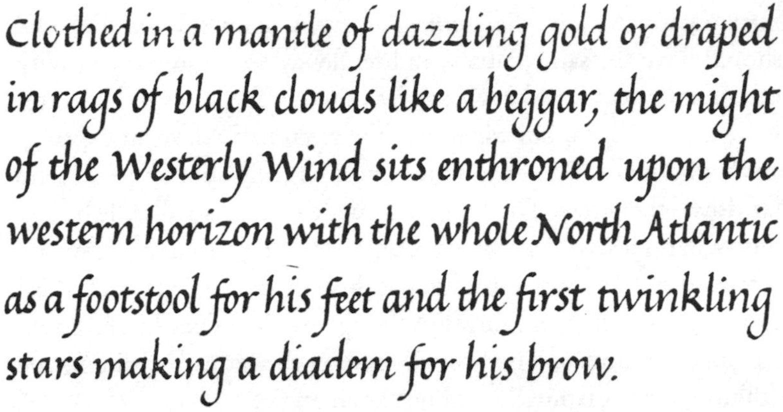

Clothed in a mantle of dazzling gold or draped in rags of black clouds like a beggar, the might of the Westerly Wind sits enthroned upon the western horizon with the whole North Atlantic as a footstool for his feet and the first twinkling stars making a diadem for his brow.

FIG. 26

(Quotation from The Mirror of the Sea *by Joseph Conrad)*

which suggests it was held to be a letter with a strong individuality. (Another form is 3)

Double consonants may be treated as in Fig. 27:

FIG. 27

There are various alternatives to the letters described. Another form of *e* is made with two strokes and although it has a pen-lift it has notable virtues in its favour: it is less likely to blob than a looped *e* and because the downstroke is a flattened curve the rhythm of the hand is preserved from a tendency to a wavy rhythm: ℓℓℓℓ The bow, rather like a canted 2, must be small, joining the downstroke not lower than half-way from the top of the letter. This form of *e*, commonly found in sixteenth-century scripts, is often adopted doubtfully at first but later is ac-

62

cepted and liked. It is expedient then to use both forms of *e*. The tongue of the alternative *e* is a means of joining and is not required when not a join or for the recognition of the letter.

The *d* made with two strokes may be substituted at the end of a word by *∂*, but as this alternative is a mediaeval letter it may seem to intrude.

The angular letters *v*, *w*, and *y* may be based on the letter *u* and be made so: *v w y*

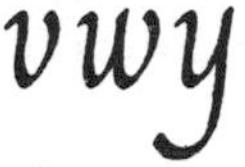

The letter *b* may be counter-clockwise in accent and then it can continue by a horizontal join when this is convenient: *b*

The letter *s* may be affected by joins: *os is ss*

The beginning of the ascenders of *b*, *d*, *h*, *k*, and *l* in the first pen-made model is shown in Fig. 21. The simple straight down-stroke must give way with the development of the hand to something more natural to the quick adjustment of pen to paper in a

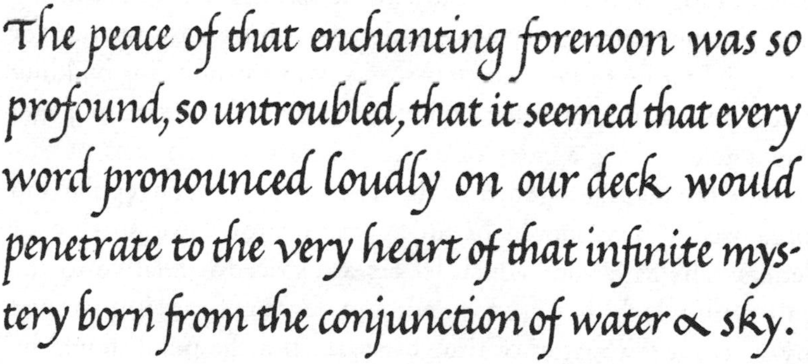

The peace of that enchanting forenoon was so profound, so untroubled, that it seemed that every word pronounced loudly on our deck would penetrate to the very heart of that infinite mystery born from the conjunction of water ∝ sky.

FIG. 28

(*Quotation from* The Mirror of the Sea *by Joseph Conrad*)

series of flying movements or to the child's (and the adult's) love of a more decorative feature. Girls of nine and ten years of age have shown pleasure in making different ascenders so: *dddd*

Plate 5 is interesting as showing the variety of ascenders the writer used on the impulse of the moment. Plates 20 and 22 give two variations in the treatment of the beginnings of ascenders.

Fig. 29 gives an indication of the relative heights of parts of letters ascending above the height of the letters *a, c, e, o*, etc.

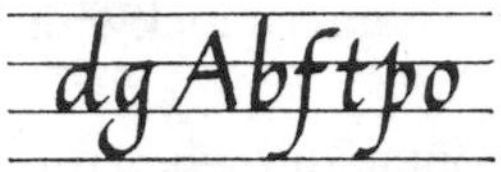

FIG. 29

SPACING

The right adjustment of letter to letter to make words is of established importance. There is need for good spacing of letters, words, and lines, as well as for the formation of finely proportioned and easily recognizable letters. The art of lettering is an art of spacing and placing. Letters may be considered as abstract forms used for the building up of word-patterns; words as the units for building lines; lines as the units for building the textual column or page; the whole making a unity of parts. For maximum beauty of patterning the placing together of the letter-units must be regular and organized. There should be an appearance of equal spacing of letters. The care with which letters are spaced is relative to the care with which they are formed; and degree of care is governed by speed. It is a matter of time to spare. But the pupil should be brought at once to regard spacing as of importance to good word formation, so that in time he may gain an 'eye' and skill for suitable juxtaposing of letters. In Fig. 30 the letters of the word

humming

humming

FIG. 30

'humming' are spaced by two methods: in the first word the spacing of the letters is controlled by the eye, but in the second, the diagonal join spaces the letters. Both methods are necessary, for when there are pen-lifts or horizontal joins the eye must take a part in spacing letters. It is to be remarked, however, that in rapid writing the rhythm of the script is a third controlling factor.

Words are often much too widely spaced by children at the instruction of their teachers. Lines of writing may be regarded as strips or bands of pattern. Excessive spaces between words will break up the band so that this particular 'strip' quality is reduced. An examination of a printed page shows there is no difficulty in reading words when tightly packed in the line. When writing quickly, however, some difficulty would probably be experienced in spacing words very closely, for the hand tends to jump at the end of each word. The spacing of words in the sixteenth-century examples in this book is worth noting. Jean de Beauchesne gives this advice:

> *And commelie to write, and geue a good grace,*
> *Leave betwene eche woorde small (a) letters space,*
> *That fayre and seemely your hand may be redd,*
> *Keepe even your letters at foote, and at heade:*
> *With distance a like betweene letter and letter.*

A close spacing of lines which would cause the descenders of one line to foul the letters of the line below is undesirable. It has been the author's custom when teaching adults to lay down no rule as to the distance lines should be apart. When general prin-

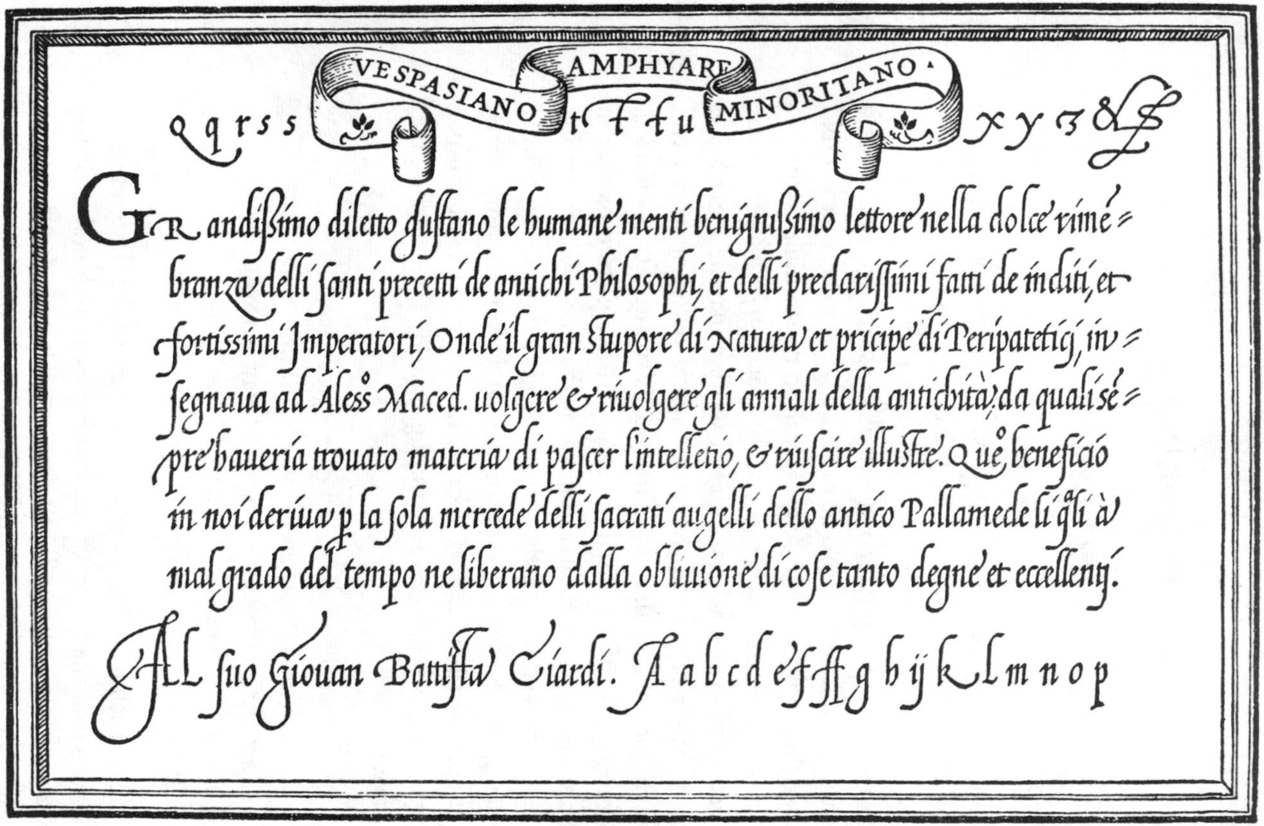

FIG. 31

From Opera nella quale si insegna a scrivere *by Vespasiano Amphiareo. Venice, 1554. Note the secondary patterning made by the ascenders and descenders (Slightly reduced)* ciples are understood, then there is room for the exercise of taste and discretion. For those teaching children, however, who may think some simple rule is essential for their practice, it may be said that the length of ascenders and descenders and the distance apart of lines might be related to the small letter *o*: letters *b*, *d*, *h*, *k*, *l*, and *j*, *g*, *p*, *q*, *y* to be twice and the spacing of lines to be at least three times the height of *o* (*cf*. Fig. 29).

The patterning of the lines across the page is so much the more interesting because of the ascenders and descenders which invade the territory between the strips. In Amphiareo's model in Fig. 31 it will be noted that the secondary pattern made by ascenders and descenders adds much to the beauty of the inscription.

Margins give comeliness if their arrangement allows the writing to lie on the paper at ease and does not cause the matter to appear to be travelling off the paper at the sides or bottom: they will be best when the outcome of sensible and sensitive consideration. Children can be taught readily to take pleasure in the arrangement of their writing.

Margins arranged by simple proportions are shown in Fig. 32 for a single sheet, and in Fig. 33 for a manuscript book.

CONSTRUCTION OF THE WORDS

For young children beginning to use the pen, the separation of letters in the construction of words, as in print-script, and also as in the first stage shown in Figs. 24 and 25 is appropriate to their deliberate practice, and to the recognition of the letter as a thing and as a unit of the word; but as fluency is developed the field is enlarged and the word becomes the unit of the sentence. In fast hands words are not written with every letter separate, and where the attempt is made there is likely to be some evidence of failure. Examination of a good many contemporary hands developed from models which do not allow separation of letters seems to indicate that the antithesis does not apply. It is then too difficult for a fluent

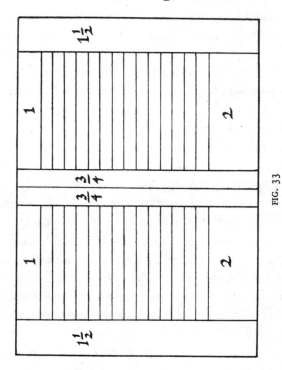

FIG. 33

FIG. 32

∧ un nu un nu un nu un nu

nun nun nun nun nun nun

au cu du hu iu ku lu mu nu uu

ne ni nj nm nn no np nr ns nt

nu nv nw nx ny   ue ui uo

am an as at in is it us inn nun

aim him hum lime limit mint

clip dip din do dun cup hip lip

ca ea cn en cp ep cs es cw ew cd ed

hen her men new ear hear mean

heat leg leap dear heed deed deep

FIG. 34
Dryad Writing Card No. 3 (Dryad Press, Leicester)

69

writer to construct a word of any length by many disconnected or short strokes or by one continuous stroke. The right method for this hand, which allows much freedom, lies between the two extremes. A letter may be carried on into the next by a join or ligature without the pen being lifted, and several letters may thus be made with a continuous deflecting stroke. Most quickly written long words will be made of a few continuous strokes of unequal length written with spasmodic motions. In the momentary pause between the strokes it is conceivable that the hand relaxes from the effort of these spurts long enough to find appreciable relief, but not long enough to cause inconvenient delay. This is not to suggest the spurt is terminated by fatigue. The length of the continuous stroke in this hand may be no more than a part of a letter, e.g. the cross-stroke of *f* or *t*, and will be conditioned more by the difficulties experienced in forming letters or making joins than by fatigue. Such natural and slight obstructions give time to take breath, and so an impediment is pressed into the service of speed.

The sky was a miracle of purity, a miracle of azure. The sea was polished, was blue, was pellucid, was sparkling like a precious stone, extending on all sides, all round to the horizon — as if the whole terrestrial globe had been one jewel, one colossal sapphire, a single gem fashioned into a planet.

FIG. 35
(*Quotation from* Youth *by Joseph Conrad*)

DIAGONAL AND HORIZONTAL JOINS

The commonest ligature, or join, is that which carries the stroke on from the bottom of one letter to the top of the next, and because of its frequency in the word and its effect on a hand, it warrants special consideration. This is the diagonal join. Its use in fifteenth-century humanistic cursives seems to derive from fourteenth-century Italian Gothic cursives and is to be noticed in Niccoli's italic. Fig. 16 and Plate 14 display strong examples of the use of this join in the sixteenth century.

The diagonal ligature is an upstroke, and therefore should be made by a sideways movement of the pen. With the pen-direction recommended in this manual the oblique stroke will be found to have three virtues in serving as a diagonal join. Firstly, as the diagonal join is introduced as an aid to speed, a sidled upstroke is appropriate because of the ease with which it is made. Secondly, as the diagonal join, serving fluency only, is of no help to the recognition of words—and indeed by its mixture with the essential letters may slightly reduce the ease of reading—it is less objectionable if as thin as possible: that is, if it is the thin sidelong stroke. Thirdly, the letters of a word will be brought into agreeable neighbourly situation if the diagonal join runs up at an angle of about but not less than 45°, as will do the sideways stroke. This is the natural aid to spacing indicated in Fig. 34.

In Plate 14 two hands by Tagliente are shown which differ because the pen-angle is different. The letters of the lower script are relatively more closely spaced and narrower.

The pupil may well graduate from the hand in Fig. 25 to one as in Fig. 35 in which no other join is used than the diagonal ligature, until this method of connecting up letters has ceased to offer any difficulty. (The terminal serifs allow some children to discover the diagonal join for themselves.) Various exercises are given in Fig. 34, and these could be extended by writing the alphabet with

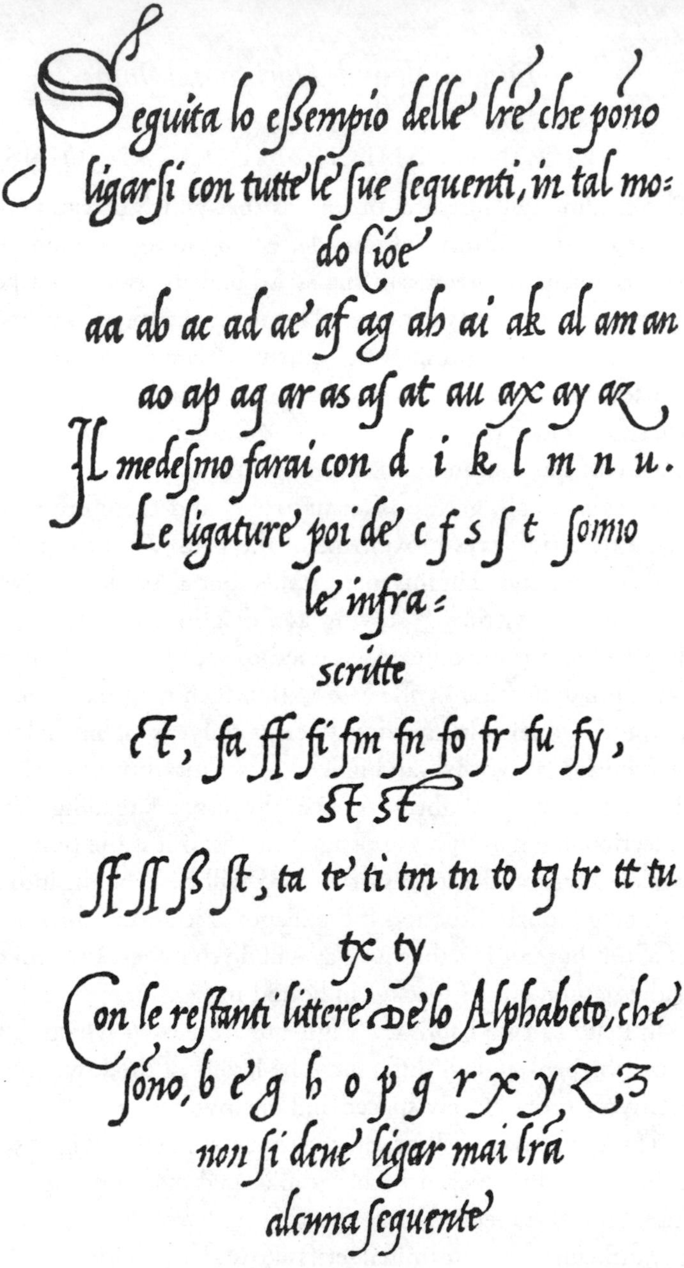

Seguita lo essempio delle lre che pono
ligarsi con tutte le sue sequenti, in tal modo cioe

aa ab ac ad ae af ag ah ai ak al am an

ao ap aq ar as af at au ax ay az

Il medesmo farai con d i k l m n u.

Le ligature poi de c f s ſ t sonno

le infra-

scritte

ct, fa ff fi fm fn fo fr fu fy,

st st

ſf ſſ ß ſt, ta te ti tm tn to tq tr tt tu

tx ty

Con le restanti littere De lo Alphabeto, che

sono, b e g h o p q r x y z z

non si dene ligar mai lra

alcuna sequente

FIG. 36
From La Operina by Ludovico degli Arrighi (Vicentino). Rome, 1522
(Sightly enlarged)

m, n, and *u* succeeding each letter (*ambmcmdmem,* etc.) and diagonal joins being used where suitable. Arrighi's examples in Fig. 36 (*aa ab ac ad,* etc.) include instances where there are pen-lifts and the pairs of letters touch rather than join by a continuous stroke.

When *n* is joined to *u* by a diagonal join there are three main upward strokes, rising from bottom to top:

(i) a slightly clockwise stroke,
(ii) a straight join, and
(iii) a slightly counter-clockwise stroke.

FIG. 37

fou oa of om on oo op or os ov own rd
re rf rn ro rs rt te ti tr ts ve vi wa wi

The thin gold shaving of the moon floating
slowly downwards had lost itself on the dark-
ened surface of the waters, and the eternity
beyond the sky seemed to come down nearer
to the earth, with the augmented glitter of
the stars, with the more profound sombreness
in the lustre of the half - transparent dome
covering the flat disc of an opaque sea.

FIG. 38
(*Quotation from* Lord Jim *by Joseph Conrad*)

73

fa fo   oa oo   ta to   va vo   wa wo

oa ot od oe og oi oj om on oo

op oq or os ou ov ow ox oy

fa fe fi fo fu   ta te ti to tu

va ve vi vo vu   wa we wi wo wu

loan cocoa cod food toe hog coin

home cone moon hop toque door

loss hour four dove tower fox toy

van vex vine voice water wave

wavy weaver wives won wood

fan fen fin fun tan ten tin ton

FIG. 39
Dryad Writing Card No. 5 (Dryad Press, Leicester)

74

Diagonal and Horizontal Joins

That is, the clockwise and counter-clockwise strokes are slightly curved deviations from a straight diagonal stroke. A slight curving emphasis or swerve from the diagonal and the letter becomes clearly the intended one, either *n* or *u*. (Similarly, for the sake of legibility, when *i* is joined to *n*, a slight variation in spacing will make the two letters unlike *m*.) A considerable help to legibility is given because the difference in these upstrokes is small and therefore does not call for much effort (Fig. 37).

The diagonal join may change the shape of the succeeding letter: e.g., note that in the word *nun* (Fig. 34) the *u* does not begin with a bend but with an angle.

Next, such joins as the horizontal ligatures shown in Fig. 38 may be incorporated. Exercises in these joins are shown in Fig. 39. Or the intermediate stage shown in Fig. 35 may be omitted and the child taken direct from the hand with separated letters to the hand with both diagonal and horizontal joins, if he has discovered the diagonal join. The letter groups at the head of Fig. 38 are to be found also in the quotation below them. (In the *Dryad Writing Cards* and *Beacon Writing Books*, however, a break is always made after the letter *r* for maximum clarity in the early stage of learning the script.)

These diagonal and horizontal joins when assimilated into the handwriting will allow a considerable degree of fluency. Although other joins are likely to be seen in the writing of a hand of the fullest freedom and highest speed by an adult, these are quite sufficient as a basis for such a hand, and it is considered policy to allow the student to develop unconsciously for himself any other ligatures he still finds necessary as increasing speed makes the demand. The developed handwriting will indubitably be individual: since humans are all different it could not be otherwise. Provided legibility is preserved, and affected and fantastic forms are not encouraged, it will be wise to let individuality have natural expression. Indeed, the rigid discipline of conforming to the

abcdefghijk
lmnopqrstu
vwxyz

FIG. 40

From Beacon Writing Book One (*Ginn and Co. Ltd.*) *Reduced* model, necessary to the beginner, cannot fortunately but be relaxed when the pupil gains speed, and then will be the time for appreciative direction.

EXERCISES

Although the author advises as a calligrapher, and not as a trained schoolteacher, some suggestions as to suitable exercises may be thought not out of place. What one would wish in particular is that the pupil should be brought to appreciate and always to remember the importance of making every letter so that it is recognized as the letter intended.

The author holds that the rhythm of italic handwriting is largely in the alphabet. If, therefore, it should be desired to make 'writing-patterns', such as those taught by the late Marion Richardson, they should be based upon letters or upon the principal movements in writing minuscules (cf. page 45). Writing-patterns, however, are not essential to arouse interest or develop skill in handwriting.

Pre-writing exercises for infants who have not yet learned to write are a different matter. Many such exercises are given in *Beacon Writing Book One*, and four are shown in Fig. 40. These exercises can be used as patterns but their function is to introduce the child to handwriting by movements related to the act of writing a simple italic hand.

The following exercises or drills in contrasting movements would help to develop the ability to switch from clockwise to counter-clockwise movements:

nunununununununu

mamamamamamamama

ancndnengnonqnun

buhukumunupuru

bdbdbdbdbdbdbdbd

hghghghghghghghg

mambmcmdmemfmgm etc.

These variations on the *n* and *u* theme can be extended by using any other of the clockwise letters *b, h, k, m,* and *n,* or of the counter-clockwise letters *a, c, d, g, o, q,* and *u.* Also there are many words in the language which make good exercises in the contrasting movements of which the following are but an indication: *animal, banana, common, domino, engine, foaming, gong, harbour, ironmonger, journey, kingdom, lantern, moon, nomad, omnibus, parlour, quaint, running, sound, thicken, unicorn, vagabond, winning, young, zinc.* There are numerous short words in the language that might conveniently be used in the early stages of learning to make words: *aid, am, an, big, bin, bun, cab, can, car, dab, dig, doll, ear, egg, eve, fun, fur, free, gas, good, gun, had, hill, hum, ice, inn, jam, jar, kid, knee, lap, lull, man, mill, mine, near, nip, now, on, once, over, pen, pop, pump, quiz, quoit, ran, rise, roar, sat, son, seek, this, tilt, ton, up, us, use, van, vow, was, won, you, yet, zip, zero.*

Related sets of words have been used in the author's *Dryad Writing Cards*: e.g. *cloud, rain, snow, hail, spring, brook, stream, waterfall, river,* which it was thought might create interesting images in the child's mind, as well as teach the italic alphabet.

In addition to the clockwise and counter-clockwise letters are the angular letters *v, w,* and *y.* Drills to embrace these letters are *vnvnvnvn, wmwmwmwm, nynynyny, vbvhvk.* To make *v* distinct from *r* when writing quickly may present some difficulty, and therefore *vrvrvrvr* is a good drill to teach the distinctive movements. Other exercises are given in *Beacon Writing Book Five.*

The exercises in making letters and in contrasting rhythms may seem to some adults at first thought to be dull and unattractive, but letters are not only units to build up words but entities in themselves, and as such have an interest which can be appreciated by children. The good teacher will have no difficulty in making the drills seem worthwhile and significant, if the child appears to need stimulus, or will invent others.

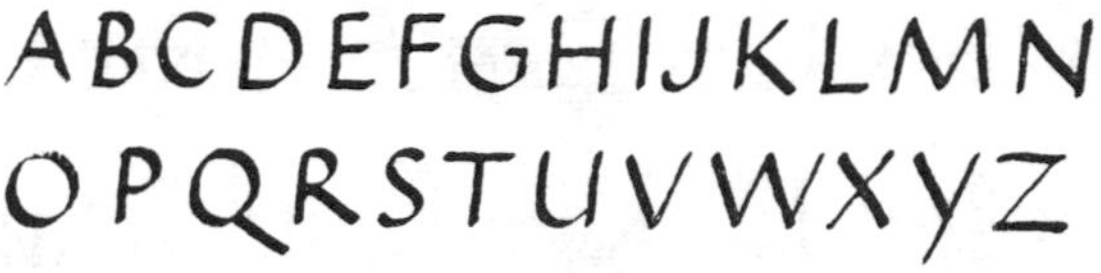

Capitals

ABCDEFGHIJKLMN
OPQRSTUVWXYZ

FIG. 41

CAPITALS

The capital letters of our books and inscriptions have a longer history than italic minuscules, for not only do the Caroline and therefore the italic minuscules descend from the capitals of ancient Rome, but the Roman capitals, such as those cut exquisitely in stone on Trajan's Column (A.D. 114), are not archaic. The antique classic inscriptions were studied and copied in the fifteenth century (as in our day) and consequently in the illuminated manuscripts of the Renaissance we find Roman capital letters which either derive from the incised letters or descend from the written Rustic capitals. In the writing book of Arrighi, however, there is a new version of the capital. Certain letters are written with flourishes, as may be seen in Plate 9. These are known as swash capitals (Figs. 42 and 43).

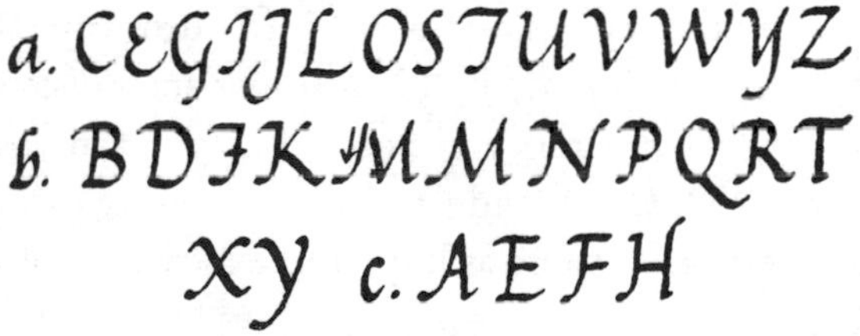

a. CEGIJLOSTUVWYZ
b. BDFKMMNPQRT
XY c. AEFH

FIG. 42

The classic letters have proportion, which helps to give them fine form; e.g. the letters are not all of the same breadth. The D is broader than the B or P, and the H is broader than the E. In the alphabet shown in Fig. 41 the proportions are roughly related to those of the classic Roman letter but the letters are slightly sloped

79

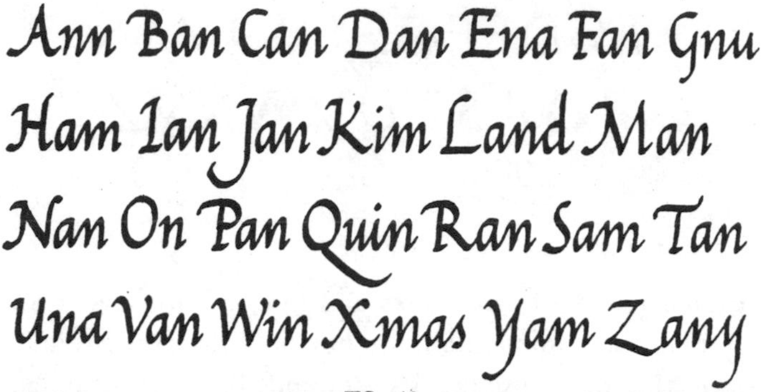

Ann Ban Can Dan Ena Fan Gnu
Ham Ian Jan Kim Land Man
Nan On Pan Quin Ran Sam Tan
Una Van Win Xmas Yam Zany

FIG. 43

to accord with the minuscules. The alphabet is a simple one and so serifs are omitted. The relationship of the proportions of the letters to those of the ancient capitals is not as important to young children as to adults. It has been found that children of ten years of age enjoy adding a slight flourish and adults generally prefer the swash capitals and therefore the second alphabet is given in Figs. 42 and 43.

The Roman capital O is circular, and there may seem to be an inconsistency in using letters that do not conform to the elliptical motive of italic minuscules. When writing, however, the minuscules, assisted by the slight slope of the infrequent capitals, have a unifying effect. In any case, if this seeming inconsistency is felt to be unacceptable, no more is necessary than a narrowing of letters such as C, D, G, O, and Q.

Capitals do not need to be as high as the ascenders of *b, d, h, k,* and *l* (*cf.* Fig. 29).

The downstroke can begin above the body of the letter in making B, D, E, F, P, and R (Fig. 44). D, M, and N may be made without a pen-lift if one has a light touch.

BDEFPR

FIG. 44

80

THE HORSEMAN

I heard a horseman
  Ride over the hill;
The moon shone clear,
The night was still;
His helm was silver,
  And pale was he;
And the horse he rode
Was of ivory.
  Walter de la Mare

FIG. 45

From Second Supplement to Beacon Writing Books One and Two (*Ginn and Co. Ltd.*) *Reduced*

THE BEGINNING OF HANDWRITING

The author holds that it is a sound principle in teaching hand-writing that one should begin as one is to continue ('*As I am to go on, so I do*'). Therefore, according to this principle, one should not begin the teaching of italic handwriting by the use of print-script since it is based on the circle and the vertical stroke and not on the ellipse and the slanting stroke, and also because it is no preparation for cursive penmanship.

Print-script, a simplified form of the roman letter, was introduced about 1916 by education reformers who ignored or had not understood the lesson which history had taught, namely that because of the numerous pen-lifts the roman hand is not potentially fast, whilst italic, its cursive counterpart, certainly is, and the forms of italic letters have been developed by speed. What should replace print-script ('ball and stick') is therefore an italic print-script: i.e. a simple italic.

Experiments have shown that a child may be started off with an italic alphabet similar to that which would be given to an older child except that it would be written with pencil, crayon, or chalk, and would therefore lack the thicks and thins of the edged pen. Such a script is that illustrated in Fig. 45. The teacher of infants would generally wish, however, for something simpler to begin with, and therefore the alphabet in Fig. 46 (which is the bare bones of the pen-written italic alphabet and one easier to write

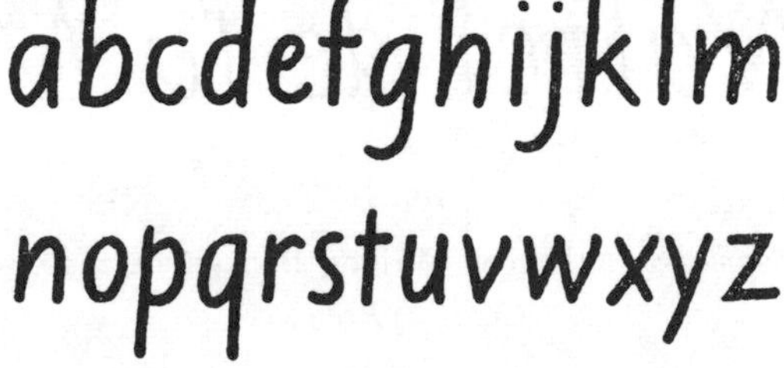

abcdefghijklm
nopqrstuvwxyz

FIG. 46

than that of print-script) is suggested. The child can progress from the script of Fig. 47 to that of Fig. 45 by stages, the first of which would be the addition of terminal serifs as shown in Fig. 48.

THE HORSES OF THE SEA
The horses of the sea
Rear a foaming crest,
But the horses of the land
Serve us the best.

The horses of the land
Munch corn and clover,
While the foaming sea-horses
Toss and turn over.
Christina Rossetti

FIG. 47
From Beacon Writing Book Two (*Ginn and Co. Ltd.*) *Reduced*

adhilmntu
FIG. 48

All the above relates to italic minuscules. The capitals of print-script are not rejected, but would be more fitting if slightly compressed and, for example, if the O was elliptical and not circular. (Fig. 49.)

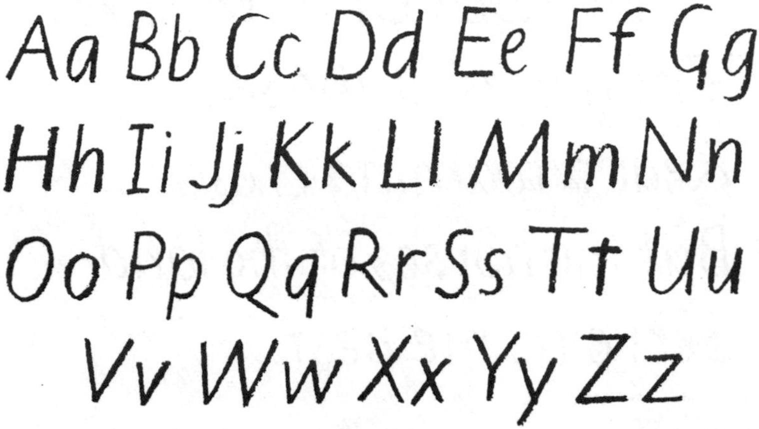

Aa Bb Cc Dd Ee Ff Gg
Hh Ii Jj Kk Ll Mm Nn
Oo Pp Qq Rr Ss Tt Uu
Vv Ww Xx Yy Zz

FIG. 49

From Beacon Writing Book Two (*Ginn and Co. Ltd.*) *Reduced*

The use of a simple italic for writing is unlikely, in the author's view, to complicate the teaching of reading.

COMMON FAILURES IN WRITING MINUSCULES

Those who need to depend upon self-criticism may be helped by reference to the following common failures:

a The first bend at the base of the letter conforms to a wavy rhythm and is too round.

a There is a break at the head of the letter which should be closed. Such breaks may also occur in *d*, *g*, *o* and *q*.

bp In the model these letters end flatly. They would assume these shapes, however, when followed by a diagonal join.

a The ascender is too short and the second downstroke is too curved.

e The second stroke joins the first at a point too far down the letter.

f The cross-stroke is too near the top of the letter. As with *t*, the cross-stroke is made not higher than the top of *a*.

g As in *a*, the letter has no narrow bend at the base. The tail is inadequate and half-hearted, and the letter is nearer *q*.

k k The first letter is accented at the base, whilst the second is too narrow.

m The pen is lifted twice and the arches are angular.

r Though intended as an *r*, it is too near in character to a *v*.

t The cross-stroke is too high.

v w The letters end with an unnecessary flourish.

y The letter is too wide.

The downstrokes of letters should neither be the thickest nor the thinnest strokes which the pen makes naturally. If writing is woolly and not clean and sharp, then possibly the nib is unsuitable or worn, or the pen is held awkwardly and with its edge not flat on the paper, or the surface of the paper is unsympathetic and rough.

It is not enough to form each letter as a thing complete in itself and without joins and to build up the words by good spacing of letters (as indicated in Fig. 25); for although that is necessary as a first stage in cursive penmanship and the result should have a very pleasing quality, yet a developed cursive writing will hardly be fluent and satisfactory if the writer does not frequently tie up several letters at a time by the use of joins. Figs. 26 and 28 are quite appropriate, however, as final models for less informal usage when appearance is much more important than speed (cf. Plate 40).

All too easily one may relate the rhythm of writing to a zigzag and it may be argued that the examples from the writing books of Tagliente, Palatino, and Mercator, give sanction to angles, but however narrow the letters *b*, *h*, *m*, and *n*, are made, it is preferable both for appearance and speed that the arch should bend over in a curve—a constrained arch but yet a curve. The narrow bend can be very narrow without being a sharp angle.

Since handwriting is a system of movements, anybody learning a new cursive hand has to overcome the tendency of the fingers to move in accustomed motions by gaining command of a new set of superseding movements. This, of course, is every reforming adult's difficulty. Those whose writing has been round or wavy in trend have to bring themselves to narrower bends. Plate 4 shows a script where letters are certainly not narrow but many of the bends are restricted as one would expect them to be in italic.

Legibility is reduced when descenders strike through words in the line below. Indeed, Sir Sydney Cockerell held it to be of paramount importance that every line should have its own territory, never to be invaded by ascenders or descenders from the lines below or above. Many italic writers do not space their lines enough, failing to recognize how much the secondary patterning of the ascenders and descenders in a good setting of white background contributes to the look and the clarity of the writing.

Economy in effort or movement may go too far. To some it is more difficult to write with a forward than a backward slope or to give a suitable height to ascenders, but for the sake of appearance the slight addition of energy required to correct these defects should be expended. The length of descenders is much less likely to fall short, for it is easy enough to flick strokes down, and often descenders are too long. Then they may tend to restrict ascenders by taking space they should occupy.

A check should be made that the pen is held so that the hair-line is about 45° to the writing-line; that individual letters are not too broad or too narrow; and that words are not too widely spaced. Other excellent checks are to confirm that the principles of unity and economy and the rhythmical patterning of italic are understood.

COMMON FAILURES IN WRITING SWASH CAPITALS

The commonest failures in writing swash capitals are indicated below:

ℬ *not* **ℬ**   The maximum contrast of direction of strokes will strengthen the letter. That is, in the first bow, the downstroke should be crossed at about right-angles and the stroke should turn in to the downstroke at about right-angles. This applies also to D, P, and R. B and D have a flat base.

𝒦 *not* **𝒦**   A wavy serif is obtrusive and time-wasting.

𝒬 *not* **𝒬**   A sweeping tail is better than a curly one.

A general tendency to use more curvature (and therefore to be less economical) than is required is to be seen in beginner's capitals. In particular the flatness of the final strokes of K and Q are to be noted.

NUMERALS, STOPS, AND CONTRACTIONS

Even when some of the letters within words are so ill-formed as to be individually illegible, writing often can be read because the words as a whole make recognizable units. With numerals, however, every individual number must be quickly and definitely recognized: there must be no possibility of error. Those shown in Figs. 24 and 50 are sufficiently distinctive to be unmistakable and are simply constructed. The numbers 4 and 5 are made with two strokes, all others with but one.

1234567890

!? ., : ; "( )" α

FIG. 50

Punctuation marks and a simple ampersand (the symbol for the word 'and') are also given in Fig. 50. The use of the ampersand is supported by tradition and economy. The simple ampersand illustrated here comes from the ampersand & (but is far from the Latin word *et* from which it derives). Another ampersand is &.

Many contractions of words might be used: in particular wd., cd., shd., and wh., for would, could, should, and which.

PEN-SCALE

Writing should have 'scale'. Scale can be measured by the proportion of the pen-breadths to the height of letters (Fig. 51). If the height of an *a* is three pen-breadths there will be much flooding of letters. If the scale is more than six pen-breadths the gradation and contrast of strokes may seem too slight. About five pen-breadths or not less than four is the scale recommended. The pen-breadth may be related to the size of writing or the size of writing to the pen-breadth.

FIG. 51

ALIGNMENT

The use of lines is either to teach or to preserve alignment. When, for example, an infant is first learning to write, it is too much to expect good alignment: the formation of letters and words is quite enough to cope with at that stage. In general, when it becomes important to add alignment to writing-skill then, surely, lines will assist and can be used until the circumstance or the occasion allows them to be relinquished. A professional calligrapher will use lines for his formal or set script but not in writing to his clients. Lines are restrictive of spacing, and certainly the practice of writing between double lines seems likely to constrain, by attracting too much attention to the alignment, as much as to assist, by helping in the adjustment of size, and is not recommended for the exemplar hands of this book. The use of a sheet with guide lines to show through writing-paper is sometimes resorted to, both by adults and children. Such a guide could include vertical lines for margins. In many lined exercise books the ruling is too close to allow room for the ascenders and descenders of italic hands.

MANUSCRIPT BOOKS

Where children have attained a speed in writing that cannot conveniently be slowed down without hindrance to the teaching of other subjects, and where, therefore, there are objections to the introduction of a new system, much might still be done to bring discipline to bear on handwriting lest otherwise there should be progressive decay. Thus, the hands shown as models may be taught for the making of manuscript books, purely for the beauty of handwriting and the creation of works of art, and without consideration of speed. Manuscript books can be decorated by illuminations or illustrations, or can be free of such artistic embellishment. When, in such circumstances, this italic handwriting is taught as an art subject, the practice will doubtless tend to improve the hand normally written by a contrast of standards and by the deliberate exercise. The interest aroused by the display of sixteenth-century examples and of contemporary pieces is often noted.

Because of the grace and clarity of the set cursive italic hands we now find versions in the repertoire of scripts of contemporary professional calligraphers, used both in making manuscript books, documents and advertisements.

THE TEACHER'S AIMS

Whether this system of handwriting or any other is taught, teachers are expected and will wish themselves to ensure that children when leaving their charge are not hurt in sight or health by bad posture and can certainly be relied upon to write neatly and legibly. These are the minimum requirements.

A child can hardly be expected to write a good hand if it is not taught. The teacher who wishes to help and encourage his pupils to write well will be the more competent if he is himself a good penman.

In *Writing and Civilization*, the foreword to the catalogue of the First Exhibition of the Society of Scribes and Illuminators, the late W. R. Lethaby wrote: 'First, we—that is, everybody—should recognize his own handwriting as an art—an amazing art really —to be improved rather than degraded. This partly for its own sake, and also because it is only from a general interest in, and recognition of, art that any improvement in the forms of the things we produce, from pots to cities, can spring up. Common interest in the improvement of ordinary writing would be an immense disciplinary force: we might reform the world if we began with our own handwriting, but we certainly shall not unless we begin somewhere.'

REPRODUCTIONS

The illustrations of italic scripts are from the sixteenth century or from contemporary sources. The frontispiece, Figs. 14, 16, 19, 31 and 36, and Plates 9, 14, 19 and 20 are from reproductions of models for handwriting taken from sixteenth-century writing manuals. These models were printed by wood-blocks, engraved or cut, with faithful regard to the character of pen-strokes and with astonishing skill. Plates 3, 4, 5, 6, 7, 8, 10, 11, 12, 13, 15, 16, 17 and 18 are reproductions of actual handwriting from old manuscript books or documents, written with varying degrees of care and speed. Plate 7, for example, shows writing probably performed so quickly as to be a reproach to most persons' scribblings today. After allowance has been made for such features, strange to most English people, as the language, the contractions (such as a *q* with a form like a 3 attached to it, for *que*) and the archaisms (such as the long *s*, the *r* with a horizontal extension from the base, and the use of a capital R for a small *r*, and of a capital A like a flourished Roman a), then these essentially beautiful and vigorous sixteenth-century scripts will be recognized and appreciated as a legacy to be profitably utilized today.

Attention is invited to *Renaissance Handwriting: An Anthology of Italic Scripts*, which has a large number of plates showing italic hands of the fifteenth and sixteenth centuries. This book not only throws light on the great variety of Renaissance italics, but is a good help to the formation of taste.

The contemporary examples are by pupils at various schools, or by adults who have reformed their handwriting. The examples by adults are specially written for reproduction and accordingly may have been executed with rather more writing-consciousness and less freedom than is usual to these excellent penmen. The example by Miss Catharine Fournier (Plate 39) is, however, of an italic hand used only for special purposes and is not a careful version of her free and fast writing.

BIBLIOGRAPHY

The New Handwriting. Mrs. M. M. Bridges. Oxford University Press. 1898. (Out of print.)

Writing and Illuminating and Lettering. Edward Johnston. John Hogg. 1906.

The Oxford Copy-books, Nos. 1 and 2. Graily Hewitt. Oxford University Press. (Out of print.)

English Handwriting. Society for Pure English Tracts Nos. XXIII (1926) and XXVIII (1927). Edited by Robert Bridges. No. XVXIII includes 'Notes on Penmanship' by Alfred Fairbank.

The Woodside Writing Cards. Alfred Fairbank. The Dryad Press, Leicester. 1932. (Out of Print.)

The Dryad Writing Cards. Alfred Fairbank. The Dryad Press, Leicester. 1935. (A set of 10 cards with notes, originally issued as *The Barking Writing Cards.*)

Lettering of Today. Studio Publications. 1937.

Handwriting: Everyman's Craft. Graily Hewitt. Kegan Paul, Trench, Trubner & Co. 1938.

Penmanship of the XVI, XVII, and XVIII Centuries. Lewis F. Day. B. T. Batsford.

The English Writing Masters and Their Copy-books. Sir Ambrose Heal. Cambridge University Press. 1931.

An Illustrated History of Writing and Lettering. Jan Tschichold. Zwemmer. 1947.

Calligraphy's Flowering, Decay and Restauration. Paul Standard. Sylvan Press Ltd. 1947.

A Book of Scripts. Alfred Fairbank. Penguin Books Ltd. 1949.

Sweet Roman Hand. Wilfred Blunt. James Barrie. 1952.

Meisterbuch der Schrift. Jan Tschichold. Otto Maier Verlag. 1952.

Bibliography

Three Classics of Italian Calligraphy. Dover Publications, Inc. New York. 1953. (Facsimiles of writing books of Arrighi, Tagliente and Palatino.) Editor, Oscar Ogg.

Italic Handwriting. Some Examples of Everyday Cursive Hands selected by Wilfrid Blunt and Will Carter. Newman Neame Ltd. 1954.

The First Writing Book. A facsimile of Arrighi's *La Operina* and a translation by John Howard Benson. Oxford University Press. 1955.

From Scribble to Script. Peter Rudland. George Allen and Unwin Ltd. 1955.

The Calligrapher's Handbook. Essays by members of the Society of Scribes and Illuminators. Edited by C. M. Lamb. Faber and Faber Ltd. 1956.

Beacon Writing Books. Alfred Fairbank, Charlotte Stone and Winifred Hooper. Nos. 1 and 2 and two Supplements. Copybooks for infants. Teachers' Book to Nos. 1 and 2. Nos. 3 to 6. Copybooks for writing with pen and ink. Ginn & Co. Ltd. 1958–61.

Renaissance Handwriting: An Anthology of Italic Scripts. Alfred Fairbank and Berthold Wolpe. Faber and Faber Ltd. 1960

Arte Subtilissima. A facsimile of a handwriting manual by Juan de Yciar and Juan de Vingles, with a translation by Evelyn Shuckburgh and an introduction by Reynolds Stone. Oxford University Press. 1960.

Humanistic Script of the Fifteenth and Sixteenth Centuries. Introduction by Alfred Fairbank and R. W. Hunt. Bodleian Library Picture Book No. 12. 1960.

A Newe Booke of Copies, 1574. Facsimile edited with an introduction by B. L. Wolpe. Oxford University Press. 1959.

The Italic Hand in Tudor Cambridge. Alfred Fairbank & Bruce Dickins. Bowes and Bowes. 1962

Calligraphy Today. Edited by Heather Child. Studio Books. 1963.

Calligraphy & Palaeography: Essays presented to Alfred Fairbank. Edited by A. S. Osley. Faber and Faber Ltd. 1965.

Lettering. Hermann Degering. Preface by Alfred Fairbank. Ernest Benn Ltd. 1965.

Bibliography

Thesauro de Scrittori, 1535. Ugo da Carpi. Facsimile with introduction by Esther Potter. Nattali & Maurice Ltd. 1968.

Essemplare di più sorti lettere, 1578. Giovan Francesco Cresci. Facsimile with introduction and translation by A. S. Osley. Nattali & Maurice Ltd. 1968.

Italic Calligraphy & Handwriting. Lloyd J. Reynolds. Pentalic Corporation, New York. 1969.

Mercator. A monograph on the lettering of maps in the sixteenth century Netherlands. Includes a facsimile and translation of Mercator's treatise on the italic hand. Faber and Faber Ltd. 1969.

The Art of Written Forms: The Theory and Practice of Calligraphy. Donald M. Anderson. Holt, Rinehart & Winston, Inc. New York. 1969.

The Story of Handwriting. Alfred Fairbank. Faber and Faber Ltd. 1970.

Formal Penmanship & Other Papers. Edward Johnston. Edited by Heather Child. Lund Humphries. 1971.

Handwriting for Today. Tom Gourdie. Pitman Publishing. 1971.

Italic Writing: A concise Guide. W. M. Aaron. Alec Tiranti. 1971.

Luminario: An Introduction to the Writing-Books of the 16th & 17th Centuries. A. S. Osley. Miland Publishers, Nieuwkoop. 1972.

The Handwriting of Italian Humanists. Book 1, Fascicule 1. Albinia de la Mare. Oxford: the Association Internationale de Bibliophilie. 1973.

Bulletin and Journals of the Society for Italic Handwriting. 1954–1974.

Opera nella quale si insegna a scrivere. Augustino da Siena. A facsimile of the 1568 edition with an introduction by Alfred Fairbank. Merrion Press, London. 1975.

PLATES

PLATE I

A balanced position of the hands when writing
Note that the pen-shaft points slightly away from the shoulder

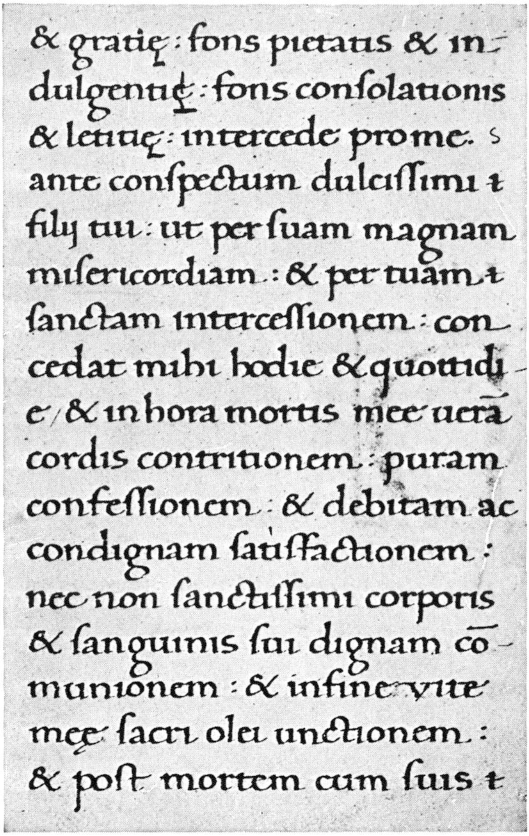

& gratię: fons pietatis & in-
dulgentię: fons consolationis
& letitię: intercede pro me. s
ante conspectum dulcissimi t
fili tui: ut per suam magnam
misericordiam: & per tuam t
sanctam intercessionem: con-
cedat mihi hodie & quottidi-
e/& in hora mortis mee ueram
cordis contritionem: puram
confessionem: & debitam ac
condignam satisfactionem:
nec non sanctissimi corporis
& sanguinis sui dignam co-
munionem: & in fine uite
mee sacri olei unctionem:
& post mortem cum suis t

PLATE 2

*Psalter of St. Jerome written by Joachinus de Gigantibus Rotemburgensis at Naples in
1481 for Pope Sixtus IV. (In the possession of Sir Sydney Cockerell)
This formal book-hand shows clearly the relationship of Roman type to handwriting*

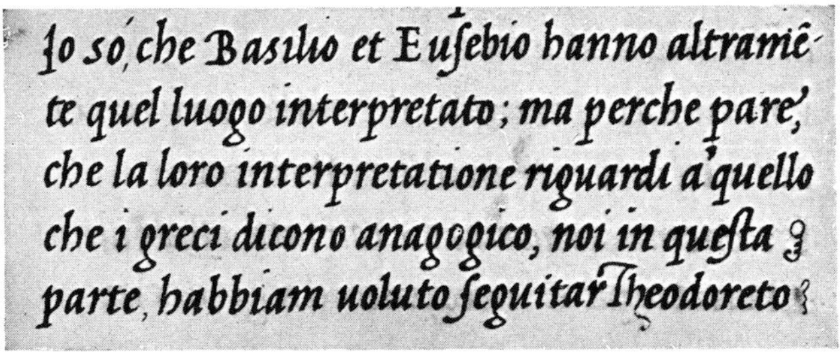

Jo so, che Basilio et Eusebio hanno altrame-
te quel luogo interpretato; ma perche pare,
che la loro interpretatione riguardi a'quello
che i greci dicono anagogico, noi in questa 3
parte, habbiam uoluto seguitar Theodoreto

PLATE 3

From La Paraphrasi del flaminio tradotta sopra il primo salmo. *c.* 1545. British
Museum (Harl. 3541). *A formalized italic book-hand of the sort described by Palatino
as* cancellaresca formata *and in the style of F. Ruano*

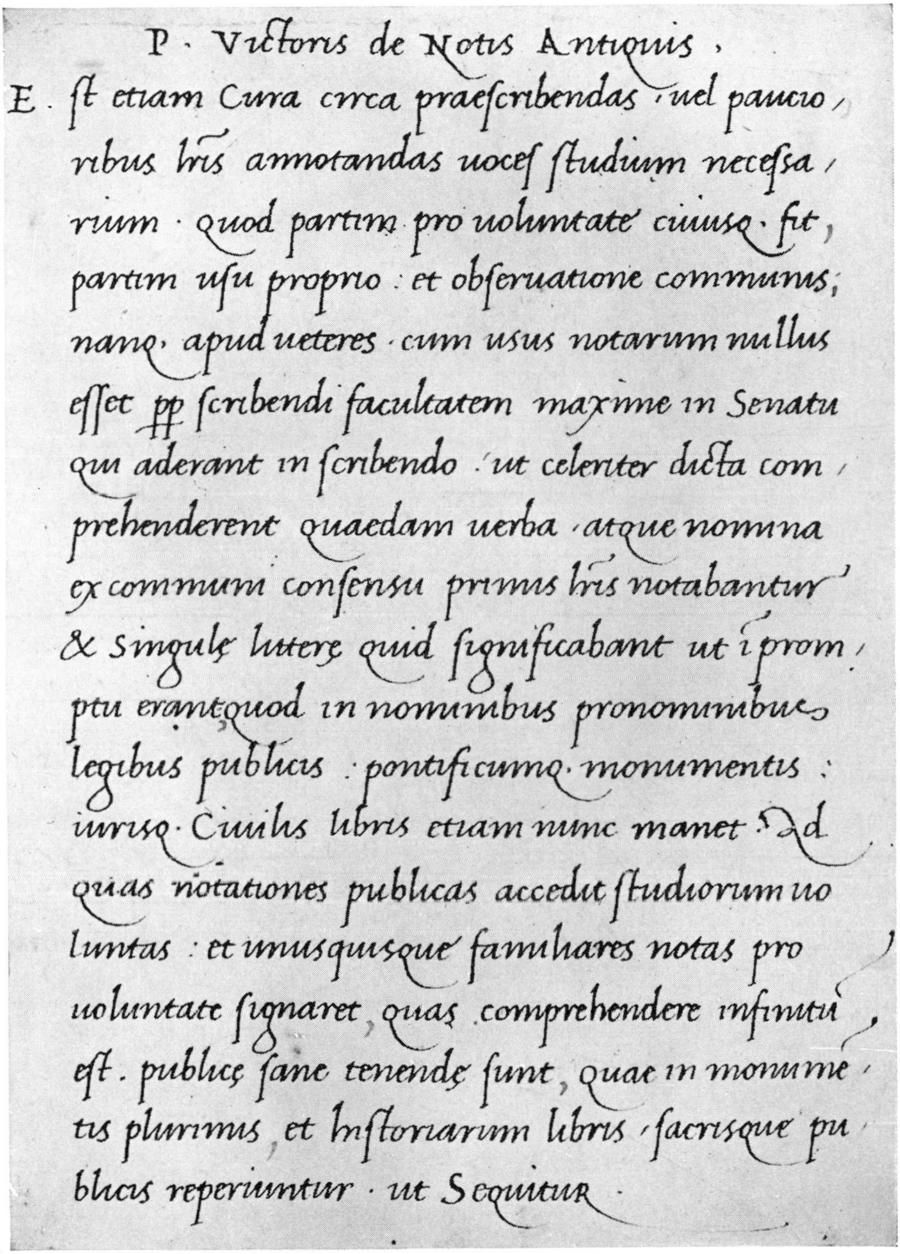

P · Victoris de Notis Antiquis ·

E. st etiam Cura circa praescribendas · uel paucio/
ribus hris annotandas uoces studium necessa/
rium · Quod partim pro uoluntate cuiusq · fit,
partim usu proprio : et obseruatione communis;
nanq, apud ueteres · cum usus notarum nullus
esset pp scribendi facultatem maxime in Senatu
qui aderant in scribendo · ut celeriter dicta com/
prehenderent quaedam uerba · atque nomina
ex communi consensu primis hris notabantur
& singule littere quid significabant ut i prom/
ptu erant quod in nominibus pronominibus
legibus publicis · pontificumq · monumentis :
iurisq · Ciuilis libris etiam nunc manet · Ad
quas notationes publicas accedit studiorum uo/
luntas : et unusquisque familiares notas pro
uoluntate signaret, quas comprehendere infiniti/
est · publice sane tenende sunt, quae in monume/
tis plurimis, et historiarum libris · sacrisque pu/
blicis reperiuntur · ut Sequitur ·

PLATE 4
Sixteenth-century Italian manuscript book, a catalogue of early Roman inscriptions

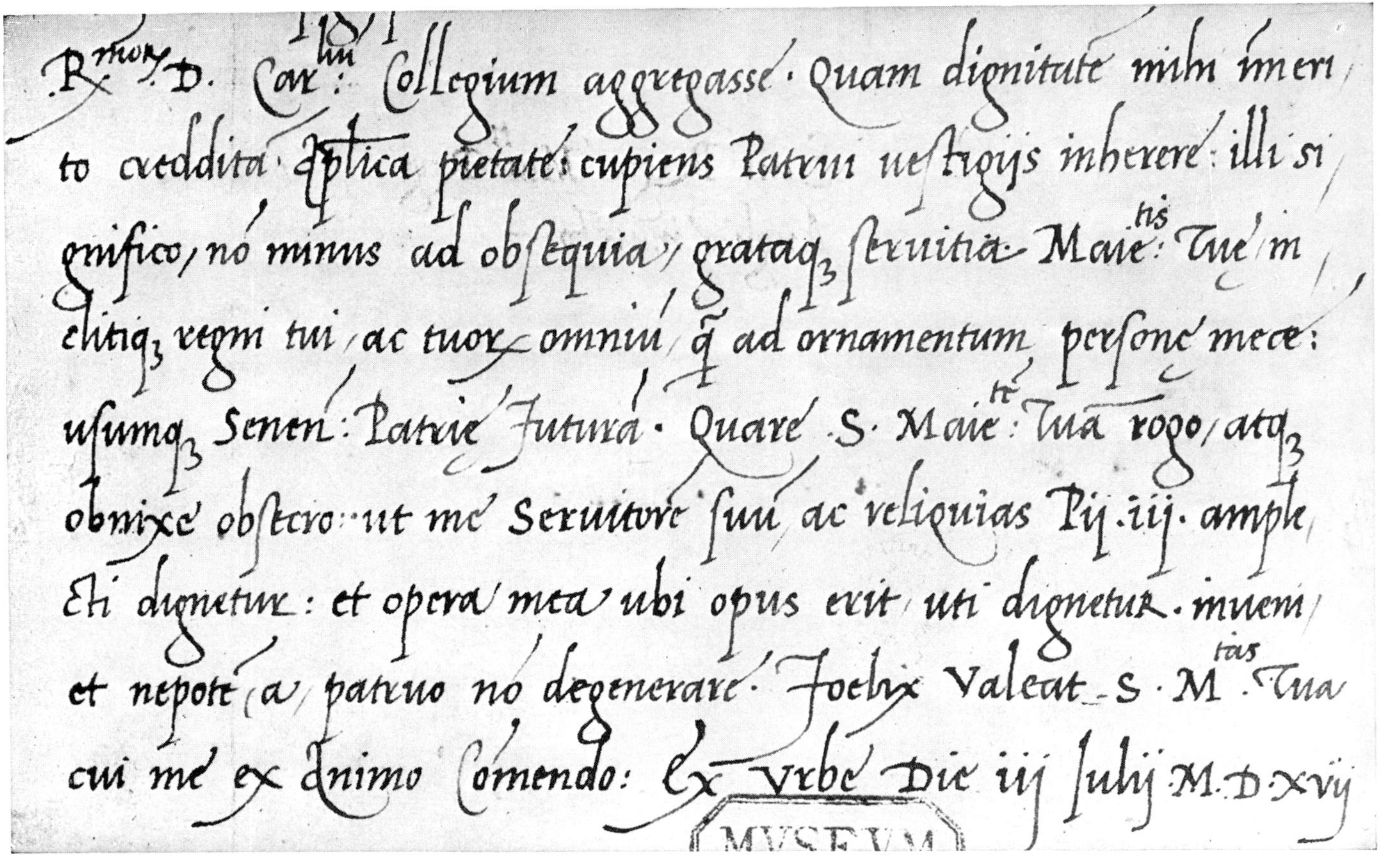

Rmos. D. Carlium: Collegium aggregasse. Quam dignitate mihi imeri
to credditam aplica pietate: cupiens Patrui uestigijs inherere: illi si
gnifico, no minus ad obsequia, grataq3 seruitia Maietis: Tue m
elitiq3 regni tui, ac tuor omnium q ad ornamentum persone mee:
usumq3 Senen: Patrie Futura. Quare S. Maiete: Tua rogo, atq3
obnixe obsecro: ut me Seruitore suu ac reliquias Pij. iij. ample
cti dignetur: et opera mea ubi opus erit uti dignetur. inuem
et nepote a patruo no degenerare. Foelix Valeat S. Mtas Tua
cui me ex animo Comendo: Ex Urbe Die iij Julij M.D.XVij

PLATE 5

Part of a letter from Giovanni Piccolomini (1475–1537), Archbishop of Siena and nephew of Pius III, to inform Henry VIII of his admission to the College of Cardinals, and to give an assurance of his loyalty, written on the very day of his elevation by Leo X. Rome, 3 July 1517. British Museum (Vit. B.III)

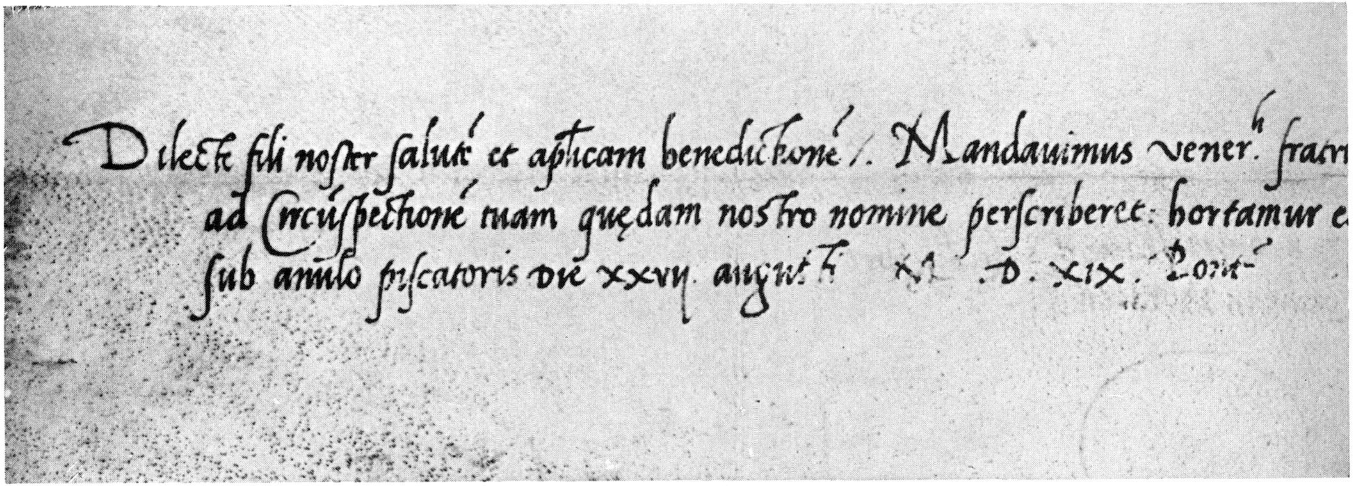

PLATE 6

Part of a brief to Wolsey. Rome, 27 August 1519. Public Record Office (S.P.1/19, fo. 11)
(The handwriting is attributed by the author to Arrighi)

et tradita, sicut in ipsius praedecessoris sris sub pi
us occubuerit : proptereaq3 in loco honesto quidem
s uirtutibus animum tuu ad misericordiam coin
ro regia dignitate sepeliri posse. Hos in hoc tam p
tum, dum in extremis ageret, erratorum memor
ali pompa, qua tibi uidebitur, ad dictam ciuita
i Ricardo Londonien seu alteri epo per te elige
nu et censurax laqueis ac nodis ad hunc effe
penitentia, quam adimplere tenearis : Hon
lo Piscatoris die. xxix. Nouembris. MDXIII.

PLATE 7

*Part of a brief (damaged by fire) from Leo X to Henry VIII authorizing the removal
of the body of James IV of Scotland to London and its burial in St Paul's. Rome,
29 November 1513. British Museum (Vit. B.II)*

i ad auocatione causa ystic comissa concedendam. Nam
u meritis placere in omnibus cupimus sicut consueu
c tua causa. cui rem hanc tanta cura esse perspexim
n dilatum a nobis. omniaq3 ante pertentata, ne ad ho
t. nos qui semper vobis placere quantum nobis licuit
sse. Teq3 omni studio et amore hortamur, vt dictum I
fore. Quod recipiemus a Cir^{ne} tua longe gratissimum
ris die xix. July. M D xxix. Pontificatus

PLATE 8

*Part of a brief (damaged by fire) from Clement VII to Wolsey on advocation of
divorce suit to Rome. Rome, 19 July 1529. British Museum (Vit. B.XI)*

LITERA DA BREVI:

A a b c d e e f g g h i k l m n o p q r s s t u x y z

~: Marcus Antonius Casanoua :~
Pierij vates, laudem si opera ista merentur,
Praxiteli nostro carmina pauca date.
Non placet hoc; nostri pietas laudanda Coryti est;
Qui dicat hæc; nisi vos forsan uterqz monet;
Debetis saltem Dijs carmina, ni quoqz, et istis
Illa datis, iam nos mollia saxa sumus.

A A B B C C D D E E F F G G H H J J
K L L M M N N O P P Q Q R R S
S T T U V V X X Y Z & & Bz &Bz

Ludouicus Vicentinus scribebat Romæ anno
salutis M D XXIII

Dilecto filio Ludouico de Henricis laico
Vicencio familiari nostro.

etiam quo alio tribuente sensit, commeo
rari. ut enim illic commemoratę. ita hic
reddita laudis commendatio est.
De Agrigentino Gillia.

S Vbnectam huic Agrigentinu
Gilliam. quem propemodum ip
sius liberalitatis praecordia constat ha
buisse. erat enim opibus excellens sed
multo etiam animo, quam diuitijs locu
pletior. semperq3 in eroganda potius, qua
in contrahenda pecunia occupatus. adeo
ut domus eius quasi quaedam munifice
tiae officina crederetur. illinc enim pu
blicis usibus apta monimenta extrueba
tur. illinc grata populi oculis spec ta
cula edebantur. illinc epularum magni
fici apparatus, libentiq3 animo annonae
subsidia tribuebantur. et cum haec uni
uersis priuatim alimenta inopia labora

PLATE IO
From Facta and Dicta Memoriabilia *by Valerius Maximus. Written before* 1516.
In the possession of Mr Frank Allan Thomson. Probably written by Arrighi.
Page size 7¼″ × 5¼″

From Apologues *by Pandolfo Collenuccio, British Museum (Royal MS.12 C. viii)*
Writing attributed to Arrighi. Vellum. Page size 8″ × 5″

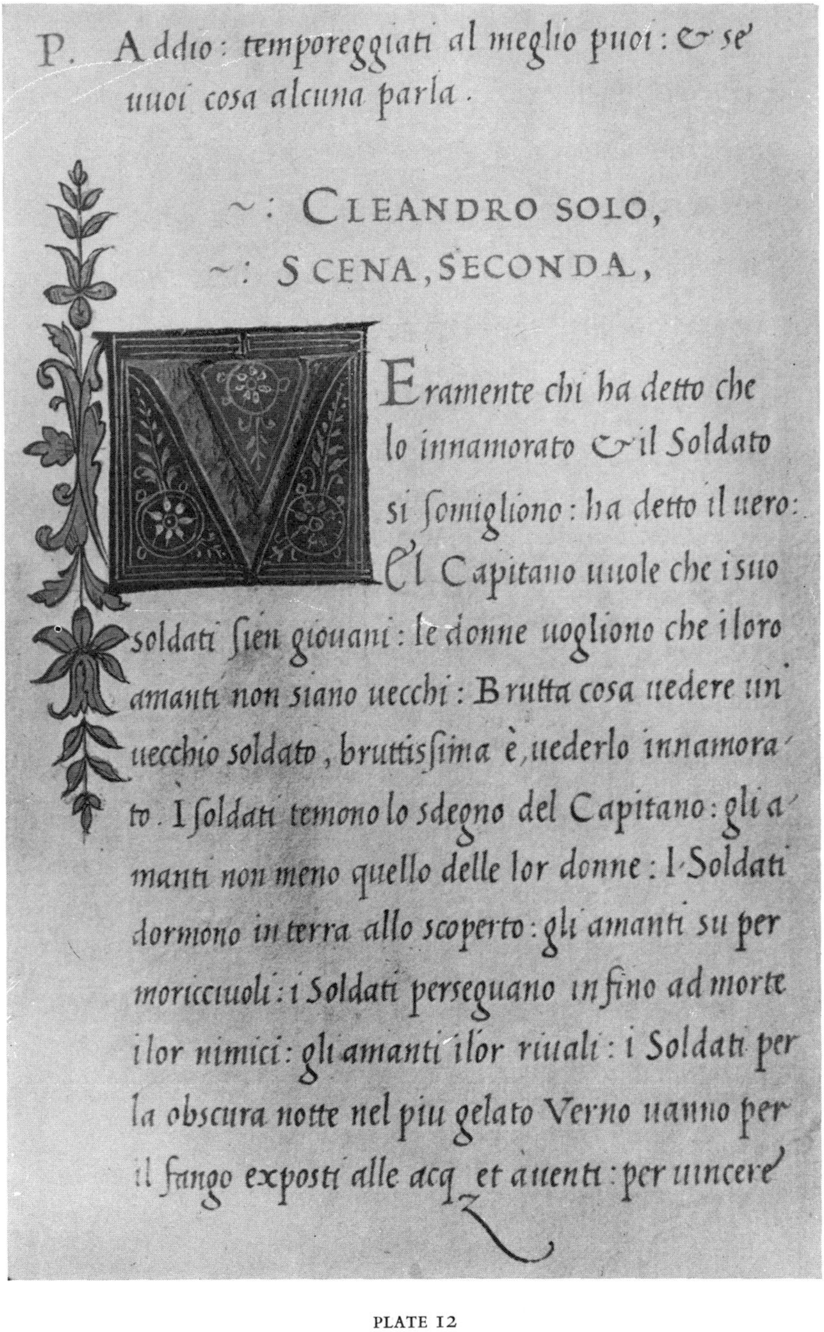

P. Addio: temporeggiati al meglio puoi: & se'
uuoi cosa alcuna parla.

~: CLEANDRO SOLO,
~: SCENA, SECONDA,

Eramente chi ha detto che
lo innamorato & il Soldato
si somigliono: ha detto il uero:
E'l Capitano uuole che i suo
soldati sien giouani: le donne uogliono che i loro
amanti non siano uecchi: Brutta cosa uedere un
uecchio soldato, bruttissima è, uederlo innamorato. I soldati temono lo sdegno del Capitano: gli a-
manti non meno quello delle lor donne: I Soldati
dormono in terra allo scoperto: gli amanti su per
moricciuoli: i Soldati perseguano in fino ad morte
i lor nimici: gli amanti i lor riuali: i Soldati per
la obscura notte nel piu gelato Verno uanno per
il fango exposti alle acq et auenti: per uincere

PLATE 12

From La Clizia *by N. Machiaevelli: c. 1525. Colchester and Essex Museum. A set
italic hand in the style of Arrighi. Paper. Page size 9″ × 5½″*

I N P S A L M V M D O M I
N E N E I N F V R O R E
T V O. Q V I S E X T V S
E S T E T S V P E R
O C T A V A M I N
C A N T I C I S
I N S C R I
B I T V R,

T S I C A V S A M
habet / ut speret in te populus tuus dñe
& in misericordia tua confidat / non
tamen sic sua spe erigi merito potest aut
debet / ut insolens factus tuam nequa·
q̃ amplius iustitiam uereatur, sudare',
et algere illum necesse est, in laboribus. & erumnis / die noc-
teq̃ uersari / ut seipsum exuperet / ac proportionem animę
ad corpus / mentis ad sensus, diuinitatis ad mortalitatem /
spiritus ad carnem assequat / et iustissimum furorem tuuz
aufugiat, Ita enim homo gradatim, quum usque ad octu-
agesimum uitę annum proficiendo peruenerit (ultra quę
non est facile filum produci) maximum uirtutis robur / so-
lidamq̃ meritorum magnitudinem sibi comparasse' intel-
liget. Qua quidem suę conditionis parta stabilitate / diui-
nę pietatis subeat firmamentum. & ueluti a primo / sen-
suum / phantasię / rationis, et intellectus quadrato / per in-
tentiores duodecim fidei gradus / sexq̃ uirtutum pariter/
excellentiam / tanq̃ per conunctissima media / lustratis no.

.a i.

PLATE 13
Expositio of the Sixth Psalm. *Cristoforo Marcello. 1523 Vatican
Library (Vat. Lat. 3643). Writing attributed to Genesius de la
Barrera*

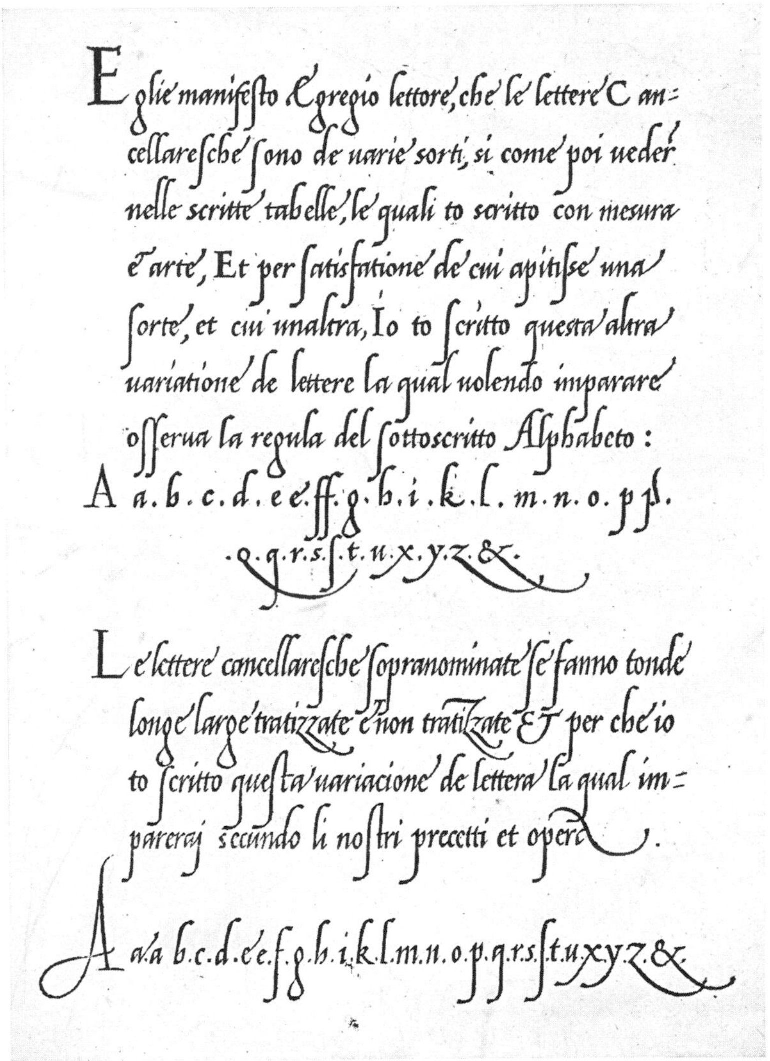

E glie' manifesto d'egregio lettore', che' le' lettere' C an=
cellaresche' sono de' uarie' sorti, si come' poi ueder'
nelle' scritte' tabelle', le' quali io scritto con mesura
e'arte', Et per satisfatione' de' cui apitisse' una'
sorte', et cui unaltra, Io to scritto questa'altra'
uariatione' de' lettere la qual uolendo imparare'
osserua la regula del sottoscritto Alphabeto :
A a. b. c. d. e e'. ff. g. h. i. k. l. m. n. o. p pl.
. o. q. r. s. f. t. u. x. y. z &.

L e' lettere' cancellaresche' sopranominate' se' fanno tonde'
longe' large' tratizzate' e' non tratizate' Et per che' io
to scritto questa'uariacione' de' lettera' la qual im =
pareraj secundo li nostri precetti et opera .

A a'a b. c. d. d e. f. g. h. i. k l. m. n. o. p q. r. s. f. t. u. x. y. z &.

PLATE 14

Page from the writing book of G. A. Tagliente Opera che insegna a scrivere
Venice, 1524. Victoria & Albert Museum
The difference in the two hands comes from a difference in the angle of the pen's edge to
the horizontal (see page 65). The pen-angle in the upper hand is from 45° to 50°, in
the lower hand from 50° to 55°. It is interesting to compare these exemplars with the
freer script of Plate 7. The hands shown above are perhaps too angular for our eyes, but
the angularity is partly due to the inscriptions being printed from a wood-block

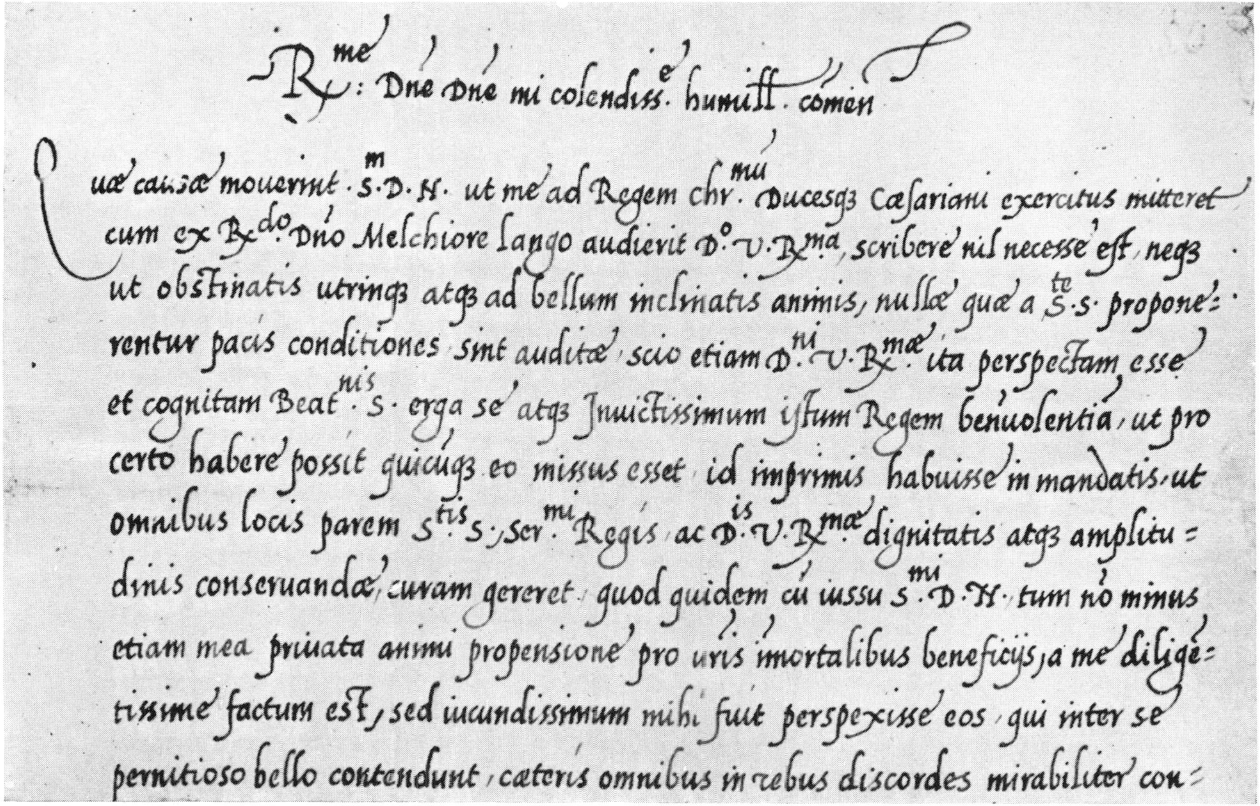
Rme: Dne Dne mi colendisse. humill. comen

Quae causae mouerint Sm. S. D. N. ut me ad Regem chrmu. Ducesq3 Caesariani exercitus mitteret
cum ex Rdo. Dno Melchiore Lango audierit Do. V. Rma, scribere nil necesse est, neq3
ut obstinatis utrinq3 atq3 ad bellum inclinatis animis, nullae quae a Ste. S. propone=
rentur pacis conditiones sint auditae, scio etiam Dni. V. Rmae ita perspectam esse
et cognitam Beatnis. S. erga se atq3 Inuictissimum istum Regem beniuolentia, ut pro
certo habere possit quicuq3 eo missus esset, id imprimis habuisse in mandatis, ut
omnibus locis parem Stis. S., Sermi. Regis ac Dis. V. Rmae dignitatis atq3 amplitu=
dinis conseruandae curam gereret, quod quidem cu iussu Smi. D. N. tum no minus
etiam mea priuata animi propensione pro uris imortalibus beneficijs, a me dilige=
tissime factum est, sed iucundissimum mihi fuit perspexisse eos, qui inter se
pernitioso bello contendunt, caeteris omnibus in rebus discordes mirabiliter con=

PLATE 15

Part of a letter to Cardinal Wolsey from J. M. Giberto. Rome, 12 December 1524. Public Record Office. (S.P. 1/32, *fo.* 219)
(*Slightly reduced*)

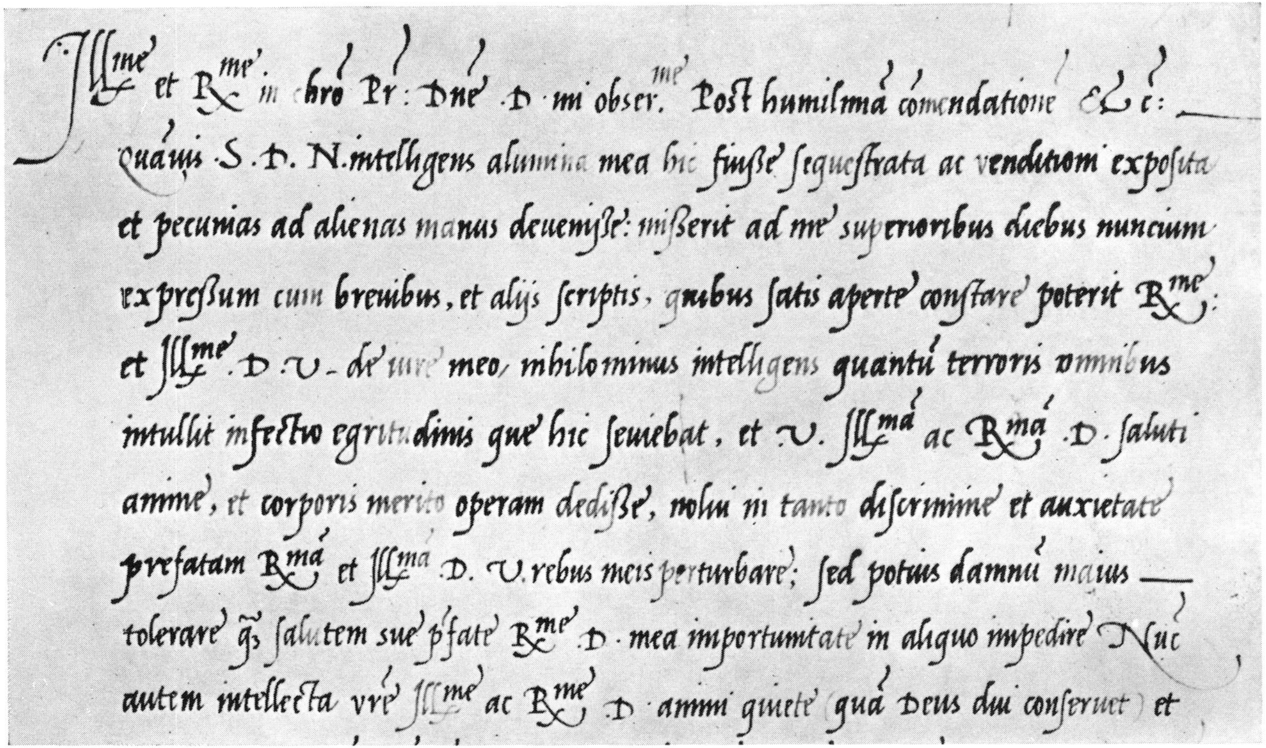

Illme et Rme in chro Pr: Dne D. mi obserme Post humilima comendatione &c:
Quamis S. D. N. intelligens alumina mea hic fuisse sequestrata ac venditiom exposita
et pecunias ad alienas manus devenisse: miserit ad me superioribus diebus nuncium
expressum cum brevibus, et alijs scriptis, quibus satis aperte constare poterit Rme
et Illme D. V. de iure meo, nihilominus intelligens quantu terroris omnibus
intullit infectio egritudinis que hic seviebat, et V. Illma ac Rma D. saluti
anime, et corporis merito operam dedisse, nolui in tanto discrimine et anxietate
prefatam Rma et Illma D. V. rebus meis perturbare; sed potius damnu maius —
tolerare q3 salutem sue p'fate Rme D. mea importunitate in aliquo impedire Nuc
autem intellecta vre Illme ac Rme D. animi quiete (qua Deus diu conservet) et

PLATE 16

Part of a letter to Cardinal Wolsey from Pasqual Spinula. London, 6 August 1528. Public Record Office (S.P.1/49, fo. 204)
(Slightly reduced)

bus etiam imperialibus, et praesertim. L. Vacuatis. C. de Dec. L.° XI. et. L. Nec
damnosa. C. de Praei. Imp. off. constitutionibus statutis, consuetudinibus Privile-
gijs, et Indultis aditis, et adendis, seu concessis, et concedendis, cum quibusuis clausulis etiam derogatorijs ad praecedentia, seu futura, etiam innouatis, et cum decretis irritatiuis
et annisllatiuis (quibus omnibus specialiter, et expresse, perinde ac si de eis indiuidua
mentio facta esset, ad effectum dumtaxat praesentium derogamus) coeterisq[ue] contrarys
non obstantibus quibuscunq[ue].   Nulli ergo omnino hominum liceat hoc no-
strum subinfeudationis, donationis, et concessionis Priuilegium, et quicquid in eo conti-
netur, infringere; Nec ausu temerario quoquo modo contraire, si nostrae indignationis
poenam cupiunt euitare; Inquorum omnium, et singulorum fidem, et perpetuum testimo-
nium Hanc Priuilegij paginam, Manus nostrae, infrascriptiq[ue] secretarij nostri subscri-
ptionibus signatam, et maioris Sigilli appensione communitam confici iussimus, atq[ue]
mandauimus.   Datum ex Aula Ciuitatis nostrae Vrbini, Praesentibus magnifi-
cis Comite Tiberio Brancaleone de Plobico, Domino Hieronimo frantino de Mantua,
et Domino fabio de Maschis vrbinate, nobilibus familiaribus nostris Testibus et c.
Die VI. septembris, M D L I X.

PLATE 17

The concluding lines of an Act of Investiture by Guidobaldo II, Duke of Urbino, bestowing on Pietro Bonarelli of Ancona the Castle of Orceano, with the title of Count and other privileges. Urbino, 6 September 1559

Like as a shipman in stormy wether plukes downe the sailes tarynge
for bettar wynde, so did I, most noble Kinge, in my vnfortuna
chanche a thursday pluk downe the hie sailes of my ioy. cofor
and do trust one day that as troblesome wanes haue repulse
me bakwarde, so a gentil wynde wil bringe me forwarde to
my hauen. Two chief occasions moued me muche and
griued me greily, the one for that I douted your Maiestie
helthe, the other bicause for al my longe taryinge I wente
without that I came for, of the first I am releued in
a parte, bothe that I vnderstode of your helthe and also
that your Maiesties logmoe is far fro my Lorde Marquu
chamber, Of my other grief I am not eased, but the best
is that whatsoeuer other folkes wil suspect, I intende not
to feare your graces goodwil, wiche as I knowe that
I neuer diserued to faint, so I trust wil stil stike by me
For if your graces aduis that I shulde retourne (whos
wil is a comandemente) had not bine, I wold not haue
made the halfe of my way, the ende of my iourney.
And thus as one desirous to hire of your Maiesties helth
thogth vnfortunat to se it I shal pray God for euer to
preserue you. From Hatfilde this present saterday

Your Maiesties huble sist
to comandewente Elizabeth

PLATE 18
Letter written by Princess (afterwards Queen) Elizabeth.
(Reduced in size)

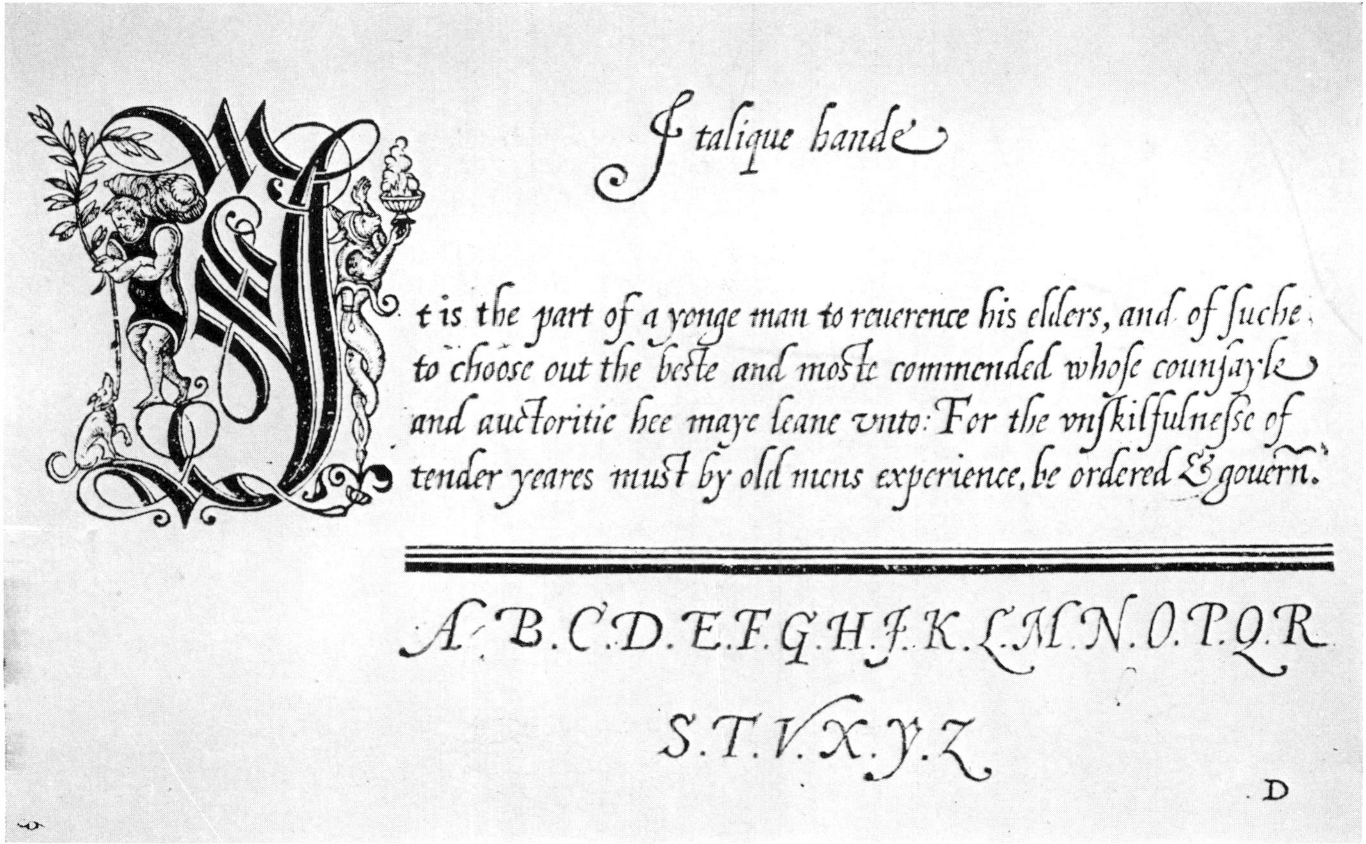

Italique hande

t is the part of a yonge man to reuerence his elders, and of suche, to choose out the beste and moste commended whose counsayle and auctoritie hee maye leane vnto: For the vnskilfulnesse of tender yeares must by old mens experience, be ordered & gouern.

A.B.C.D.E.F.G.H.F.K.L.M.N.O.P.Q.R. S.T.V.X.Y.Z.

PLATE 19

From A Booke Containing Divers Sortes of Hands by Jean de Beauchesne and John Baildon. London, 1571. British Museum

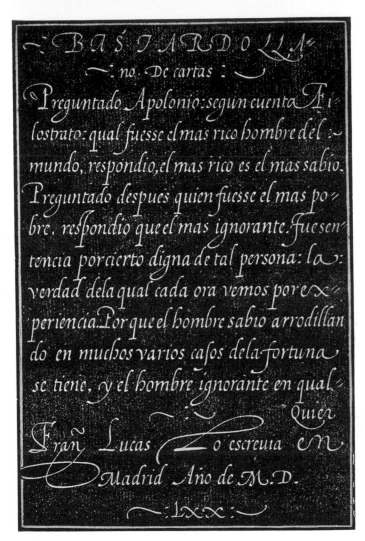

PLATE 20

Page from the writing book of Francisco Lucas Arte de escrivir. *Madrid, 1577*
Victoria & Albert Museum

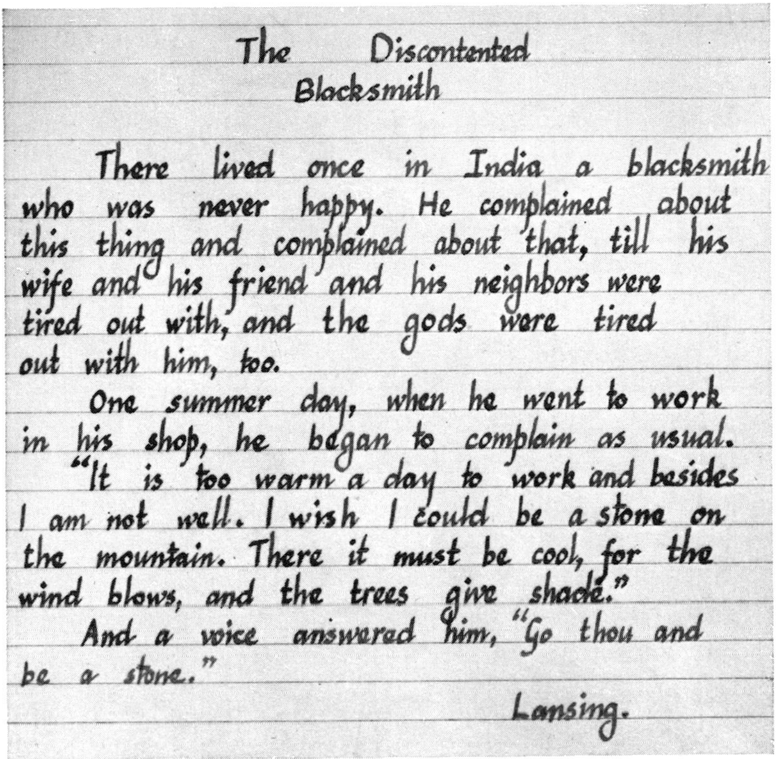

The Discontented Blacksmith

There lived once in India a blacksmith who was never happy. He complained about this thing and complained about that, till his wife and his friend and his neighbors were tired out with, and the gods were tired out with him, too.

One summer day, when he went to work in his shop, he began to complain as usual. "It is too warm a day to work and besides I am not well. I wish I could be a stone on the mountain. There it must be cool, for the wind blows, and the trees give shade."

And a voice answered him, "Go thou and be a stone."

Lansing.

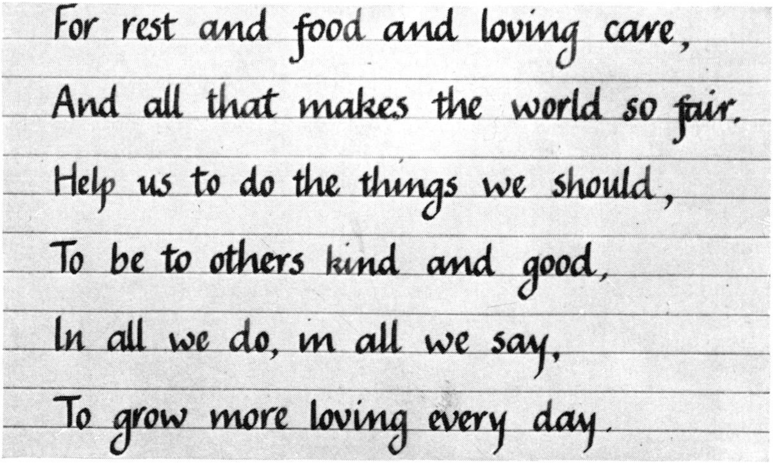

For rest and food and loving care,

And all that makes the world so fair.

Help us to do the things we should,

To be to others kind and good,

In all we do, in all we say,

To grow more loving every day.

PLATES 21 AND 22
Writing by girls of Barking Schools. 1938

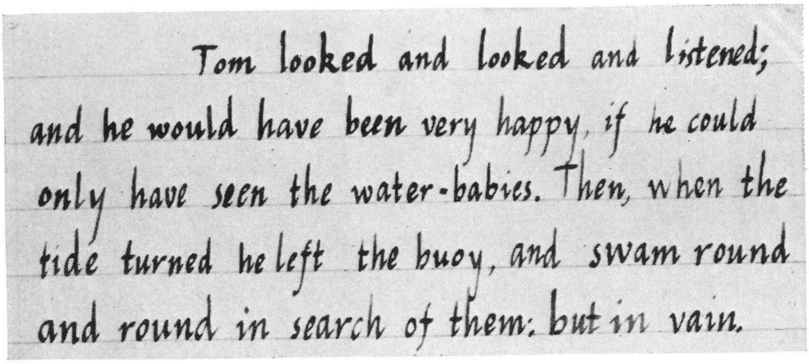

Tom looked and looked and listened;
and he would have been very happy, if he could
only have seen the water-babies. Then, when the
tide turned he left the buoy, and swam round
and round in search of them: but in vain.

PLATE 23

Writing by Carole Basdell, at age of 8. Brentside Primary School, Ealing

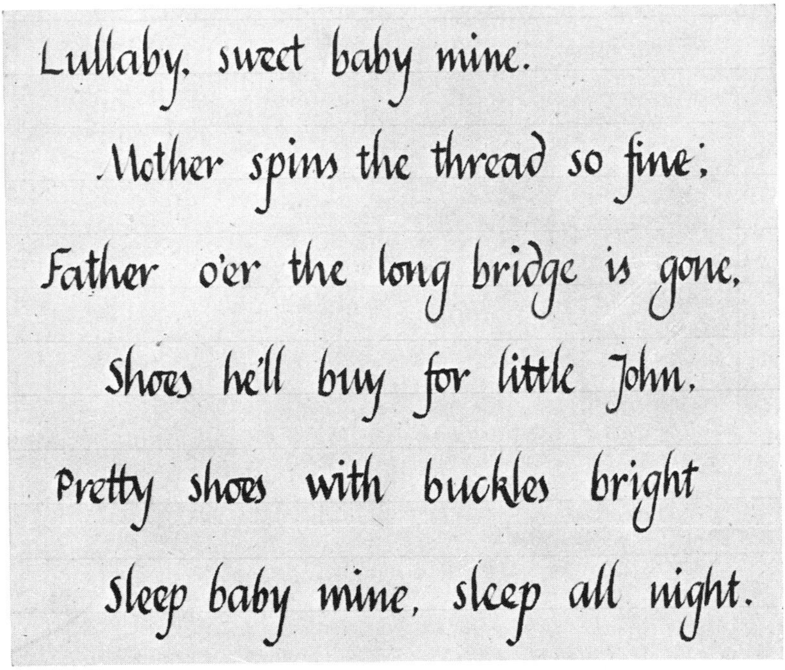

Lullaby, sweet baby mine.

Mother spins the thread so fine;

Father o'er the long bridge is gone,

Shoes he'll buy for little John,

Pretty shoes with buckles bright

Sleep baby mine, sleep all night.

PLATE 24

Writing by Barbara Fellows, at age of 9. Brentside Primary School, Ealing

And all the city was gathered together at the door. And he healed many that were sick of divers diseases, and cast out many devils; and suffered not the devils to speak, because they knew him.

He saw great spiders there, with crowns and
their backs, who sat in the middle of their web
saw Tom coming, shook them so fast that the
Then he saw lizards, brown, and grey, and gre
were snakes, and would sting him: but they w
as he, and shot away into the heath. And th
saw a pretty sight – a great brown sharp-nosed
tag to her brush, and round her, four or five

Then up rose Mrs. Cratchit, dressed out but
bravely in a twice turned gown, but bright
in ribbons. which are cheap and make a
goodly show for sixpence; and she laid the
cloth, helped by Belinda Cratchit second of
her daughters also brave in ribbons; while
Master Peter Cratchit plunged a fork into the
saucepan of potatoes.

Writing by Carole Wells, Brentside Primary School, Ealing, when aged 9. (Reduced)

God is our refuge and strength,
a very present help in trouble.
Therefore will we not fear, though
the earth be removed, and
though the mountains be carried
into the midst of the sea.

Writing by Carole Wells, when aged 10

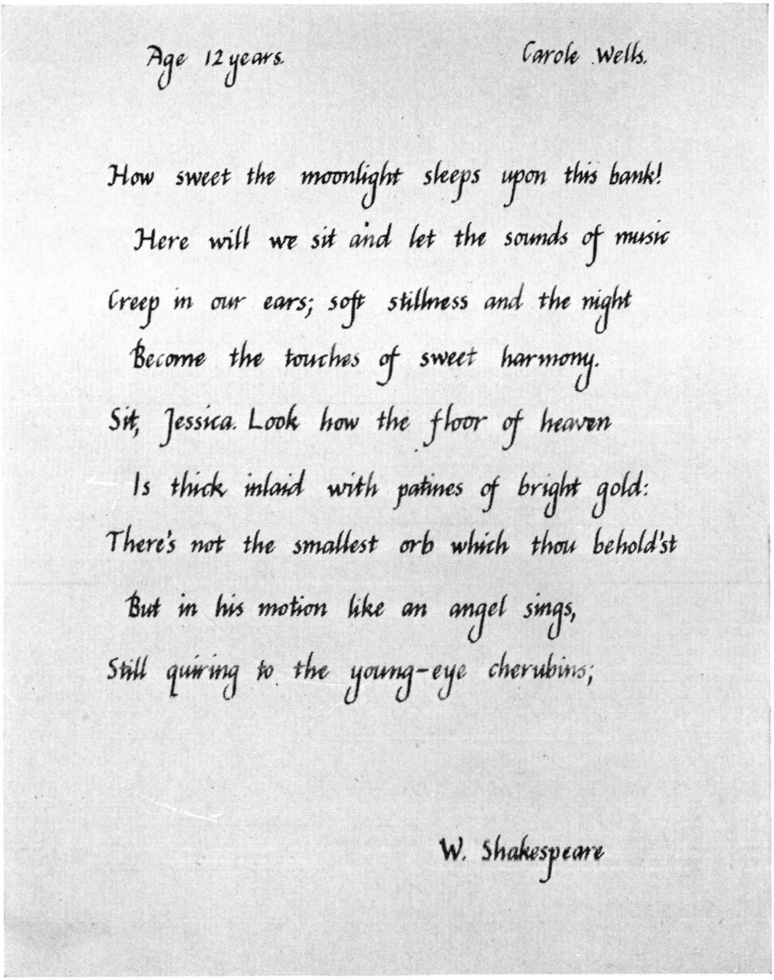

Age 12 years.   Carole Wells.

How sweet the moonlight sleeps upon this bank!

Here will we sit and let the sounds of music

Creep in our ears; soft stillness and the night

Become the touches of sweet harmony.

Sit, Jessica. Look how the floor of heaven

Is thick inlaid with patines of bright gold:

There's not the smallest orb which thou behold'st

But in his motion like an angel sings,

Still quiring to the young-eye cherubins;

W. Shakespeare

PLATE 29

By this and the two previous plates the development of a child's handwriting is indicated
(Reduced)

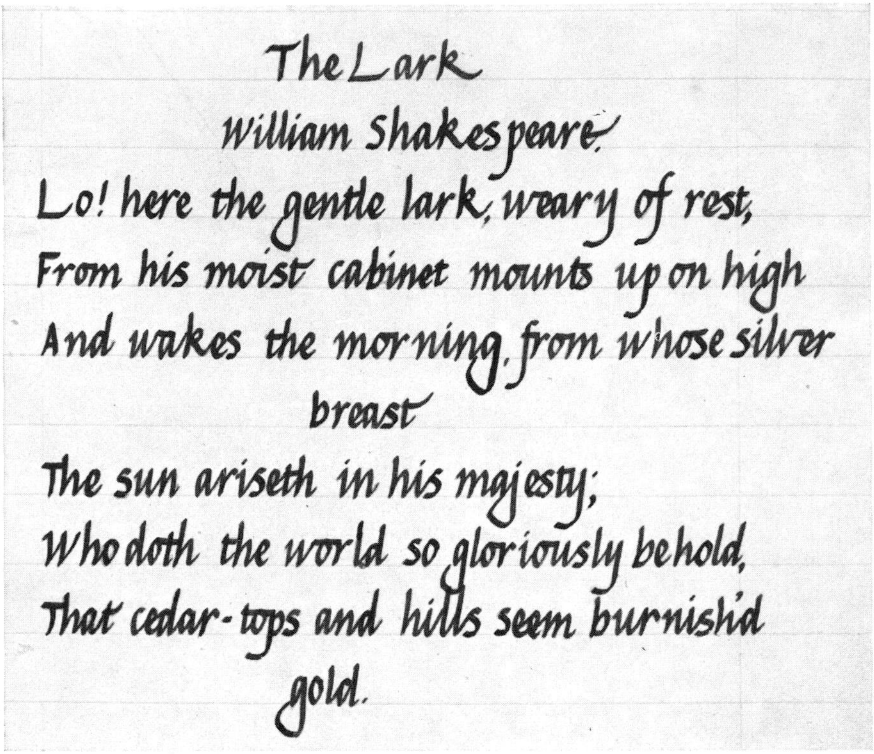

The Lark
William Shakespeare

Lo! here the gentle lark, weary of rest,
From his moist cabinet mounts up on high
And wakes the morning, from whose silver
breast
The sun ariseth in his majesty;
Who doth the world so gloriously behold,
That cedar-tops and hills seem burnish'd
gold.

PLATE 30
Jonathan at age of nine

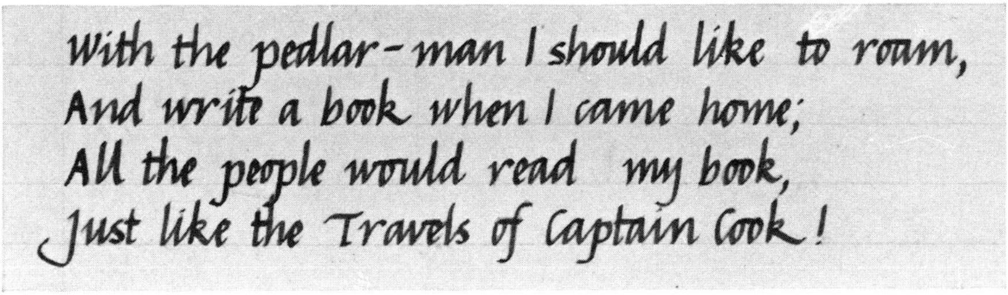

With the pedlar-man I should like to roam,
And write a book when I came home;
All the people would read my book,
Just like the Travels of Captain Cook !

PLATE 31
Richard at age of eleven

PLATES 30 and 31
Writing by the sons of Mr Kenneth C. Yates-Smith of Frittenden School, Cranbrook.
Mr Yates-Smith is the author of Italigraph Handwriting (Philip and Tacey)
(Reduced)

The Avalanche
Chapter I.

"Oh, I say, Di, isn't this exciting!" cried Jean Raynor, joining her sister on the bed.

"Yes, Jean, it is, only don't be too excited, it's three days yet," replied Diana Jackson, surveying her bright-eyed sister anxiously.

"I know," sighed Jean. "Three days seems such a long time."

The two sisters, or, rather, adopted sisters, were quite different from each other in some ways. Jean had clear-cut features with dark eyebrows, dancing brown eyes and short, straight, dark brown hair. She was the younger of the two girls, being only 14½ and was not very careful about things. She was always tearing her clothes as she was a tomboy and she

Ian Ebbage age 12 Highgate Junior School

This royal throne of kings, this sceptred isle,
This earth of majesty, this seat of Mars,
This other Eden, demi-paradise,
This fortress built by Nature for herself
Against infection and the hand of war;
This happy breed of men, this little world,
This precious stone set in the silver sea,
Which serves it in the office of a wall,
Or as a moat defensive to a house,
Against the envy of less happier lands;
This blessed plot, this earth, this realm,
    this England.

William Shakespeare

PLATE 33

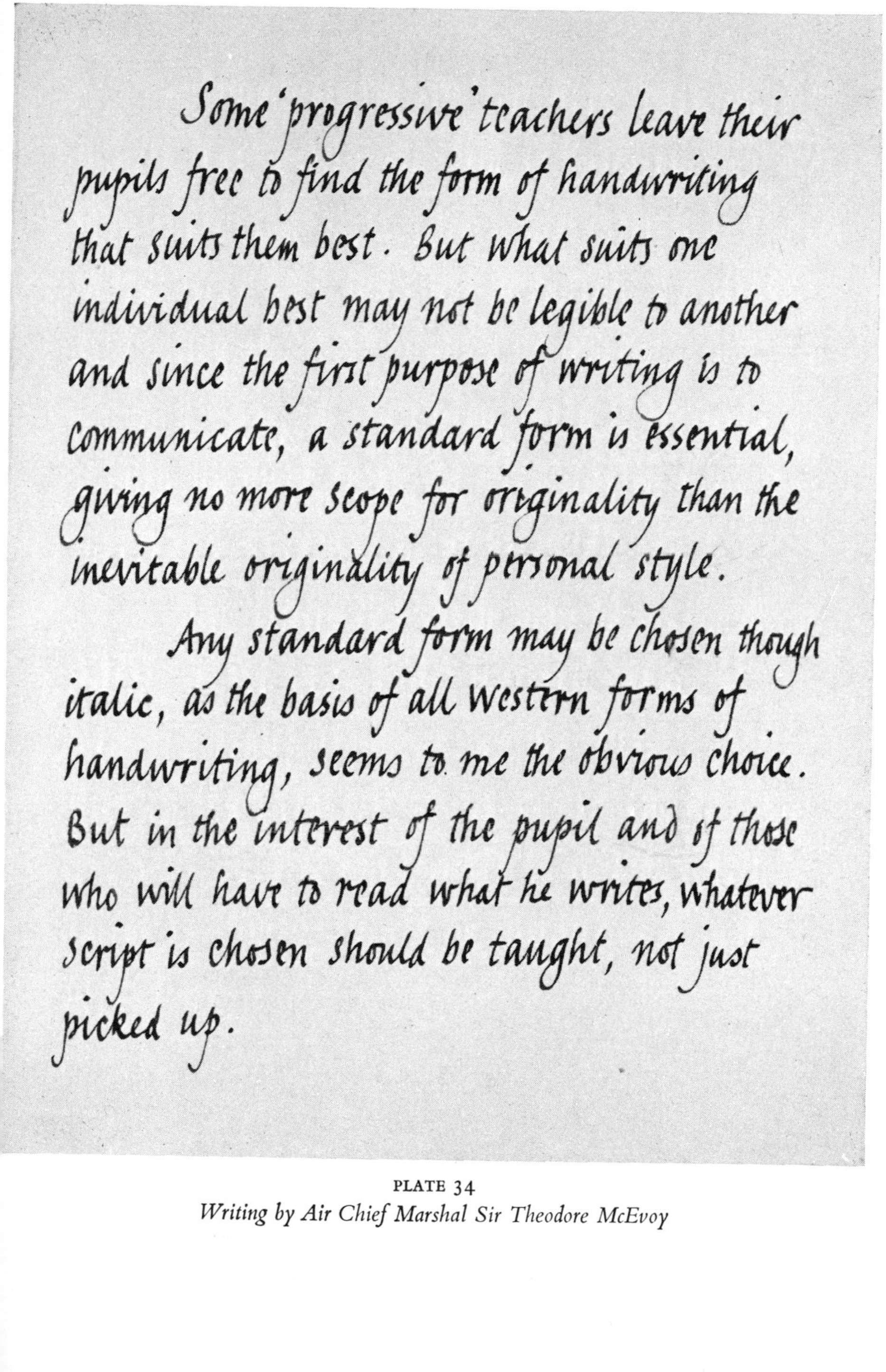

Some 'progressive' teachers leave their
pupils free to find the form of handwriting
that suits them best. But what suits one
individual best may not be legible to another
and since the first purpose of writing is to
communicate, a standard form is essential,
giving no more scope for originality than the
inevitable originality of personal style.

Any standard form may be chosen though
italic, as the basis of all Western forms of
handwriting, seems to me the obvious choice.
But in the interest of the pupil and of those
who will have to read what he writes, whatever
script is chosen should be taught, not just
picked up.

PLATE 34
Writing by Air Chief Marshal Sir Theodore McEvoy

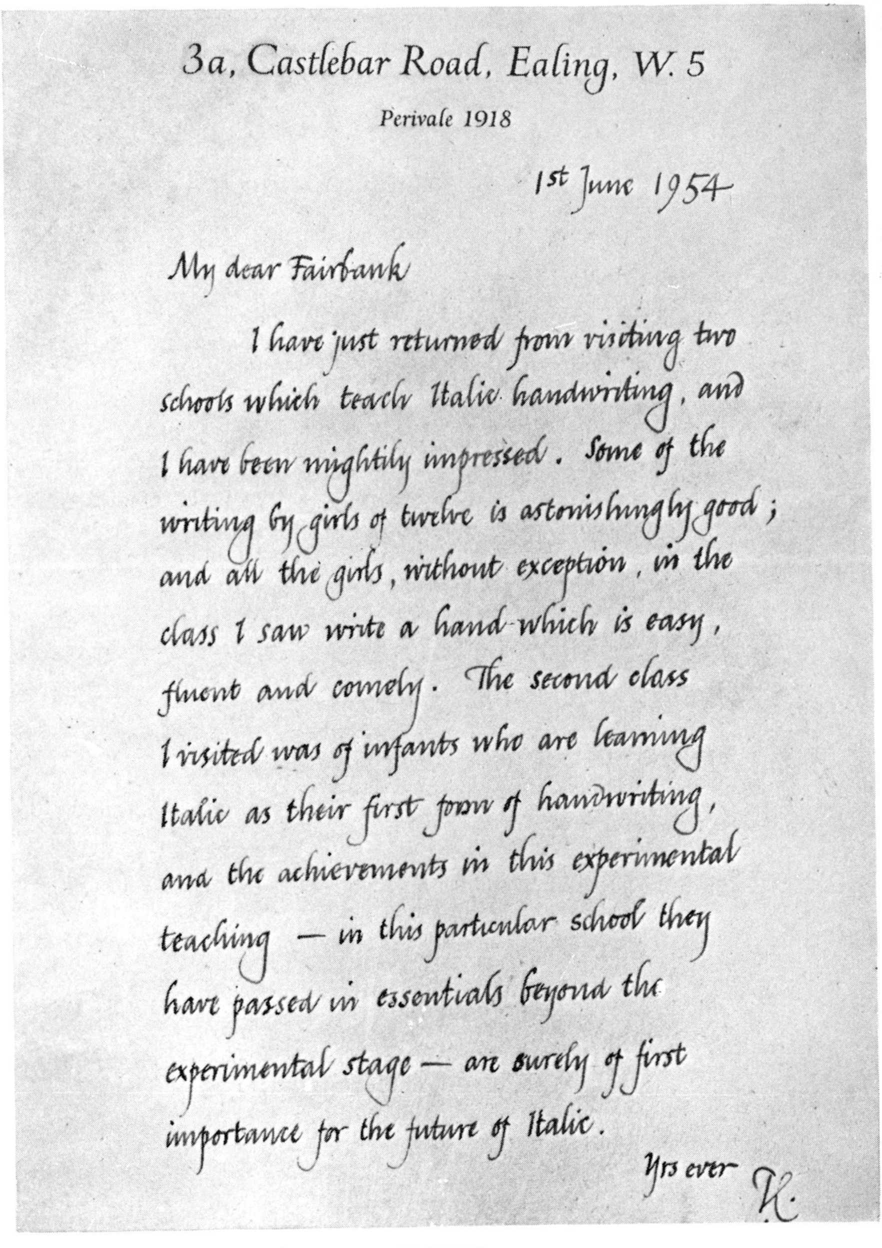

3a, Castlebar Road, Ealing, W. 5

Perivale 1918

1st June 1954

My dear Fairbank

I have just returned from visiting two schools which teach Italic handwriting, and I have been mightily impressed. Some of the writing by girls of twelve is astonishingly good; and all the girls, without exception, in the class I saw write a hand which is easy, fluent and comely. The second class I visited was of infants who are learning Italic as their first form of handwriting, and the achievements in this experimental teaching — in this particular school they have passed in essentials beyond the experimental stage — are surely of first importance for the future of Italic.

Yrs ever

H.

PLATE 35
Writing by the late Joseph Compton

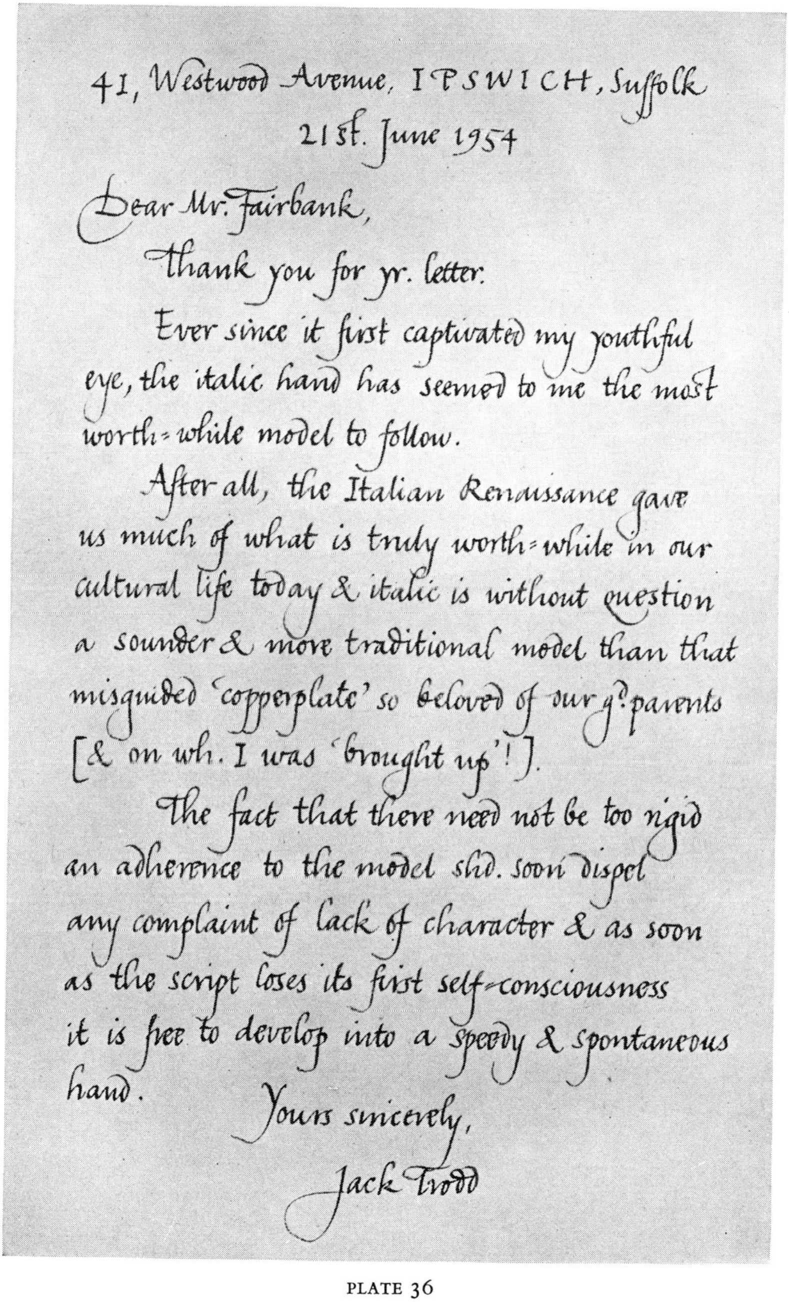

41, Westwood Avenue, IPSWICH, Suffolk
21st. June 1954

Dear Mr. Fairbank,

thank you for yr. letter.

Ever since it first captivated my youthful eye, the italic hand has seemed to me the most worth-while model to follow.

After all, the Italian Renaissance gave us much of what is truly worth-while in our cultural life today & italic is without question a sounder & more traditional model than that misguided 'copperplate' so beloved of our g?parents [& on wh. I was 'brought up'!].

The fact that there need not be too rigid an adherence to the model shd. soon dispel any complaint of lack of character & as soon as the script loses its first self-consciousness it is free to develop into a speedy & spontaneous hand.

Yours sincerely,

Jack Trodd

PLATE 36
Writing by Mr J. S. T. Trodd. (Slightly reduced)

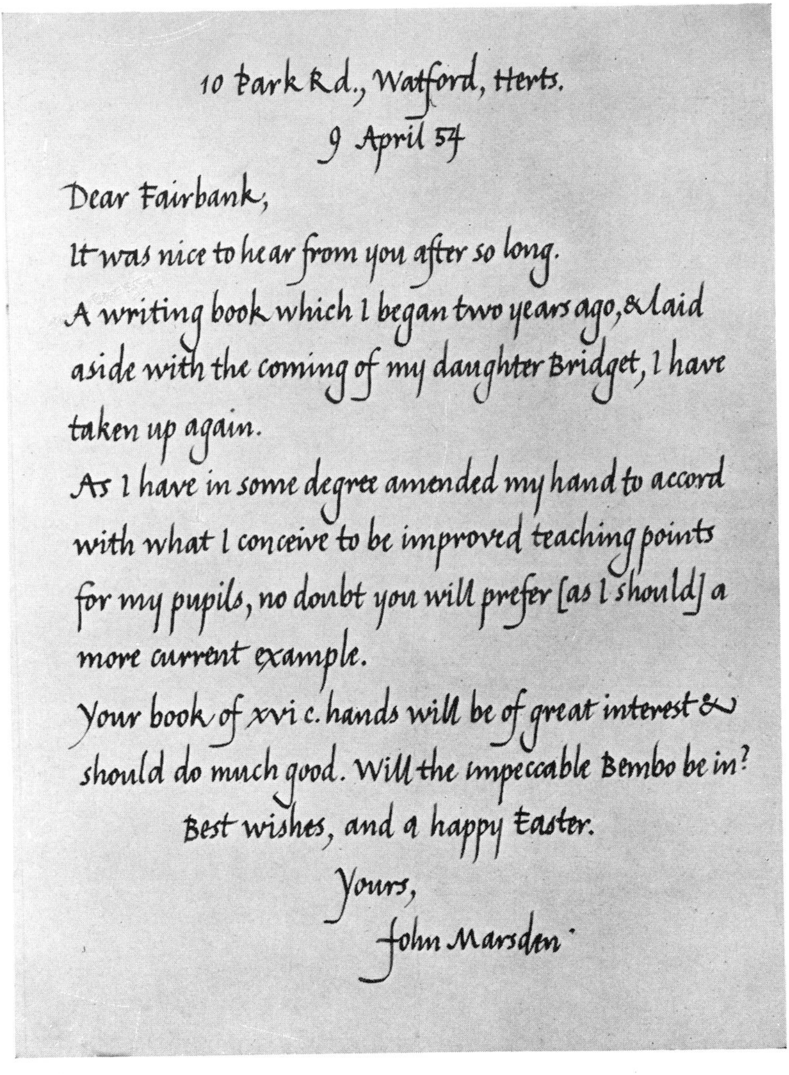

10 Park Rd., Watford, Herts.

9 April 54

Dear Fairbank,

It was nice to hear from you after so long.

A writing book which I began two years ago, & laid aside with the coming of my daughter Bridget, I have taken up again.

As I have in some degree amended my hand to accord with what I conceive to be improved teaching points for my pupils, no doubt you will prefer [as I should] a more current example.

Your book of xvi c. hands will be of great interest & should do much good. Will the impeccable Bembo be in?

Best wishes, and a happy Easter.

Yours,

John Marsden

PLATE 37
Writing by Mr John Marsden. (Reduced)

1384 Troy Avenue, Brooklyn 3, N.Y.

14 January 1961

Dear Mr. Fairbank,

How fortunate I was to see your 'Plato' written out by Edward Johnston! I felt so at the time, but now I know my privilege more, for I've just read Priscilla Johnston's biography of her father. What a delightful book! And how much it tells about that remarkable man who was there to blow on a flame that William Morris kindled, and eventually to make such a lovely light.

It is hard for us to realize now how much we owe to Johnston. This book makes clear the debt, & gives us besides a wonderfully sympathetic picture of a craftsman who seemed to know First Things intuitively.

Yours sincerely,

Catharine Fournier

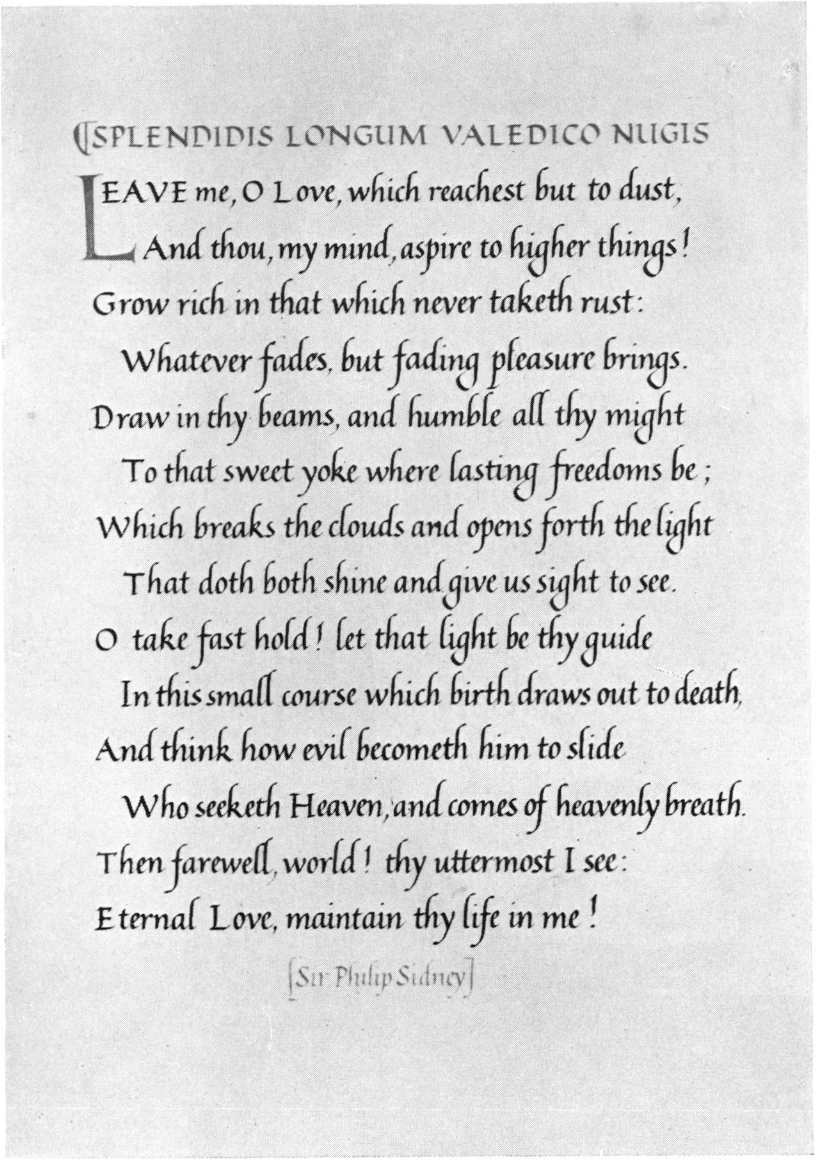

⟨SPLENDIDIS LONGUM VALEDICO NUGIS

LEAVE me, O Love, which reachest but to dust,
    And thou, my mind, aspire to higher things!
Grow rich in that which never taketh rust:
    Whatever fades, but fading pleasure brings.
Draw in thy beams, and humble all thy might
    To that sweet yoke where lasting freedoms be;
Which breaks the clouds and opens forth the light
    That doth both shine and give us sight to see.
O take fast hold! let that light be thy guide
    In this small course which birth draws out to death,
And think how evil becometh him to slide
    Who seeketh Heaven, and comes of heavenly breath.
Then farewell, world! thy uttermost I see:
Eternal Love, maintain thy life in me!

[Sir Philip Sidney]

PLATE 39

Sonnet written in red and black by Alfred Fairbank. 1936. In the possession of Miss Dorothy Hutton. A careful script, without joins, written for mural decoration

'I wd. suggest...that the perpendicular upright, which is much the most satisfactory when one contemplates the letters individually, is undesirable in a script, since any, even the slightest, variation from it is immediately detected by the eye, so that the scribe is almost forced into that deadly parallelism which mars so many 15th century Gothic manuscripts. Where, on the other hand, there is a slight inclination of uprights, variety of movement is possible without suggesting too clearly the departure from a norm.'

Roger Fry: from S. P. E. Tract no. xxiii, 'English Handwriting', Oxford Univ. Press, 1926

To study the finest scripts and models, to imbibe the principles of italic handwriting, and to aim at a good personal standard, are the means by which one may develop an elegant and satisfying italic hand. The standard or ideal will be individually discerned subject to whatever ideas one has of excellence, and will be achieved through personal, skilful capacity. Necessarily it will be offset at times in quality by the demanding pressure of the occasion and the rapid passage of time.

The italic hand gives promise of both pattern & legibility: that is, it appeals aescethically and communicates thought. Through its ligatures it has the advantage of producing a rhythmic nobility that aids fluency.

PLATE 41
Writing by Miss Vera Law

Teachers should set a good example! They should select the finest models, thoroughly understand them and be able to demonstrate them precisely. This requires taste, penetration and manual skill. The first may be guided and developed: the second is the ability to discern fundamentals. Calligraphic competence results from application and determination, and demands no special gifts.

A teacher's quality consists of these three attributes and a flair for communicating instruction and enthusiasm. Character is necessary in a good hand but a teacher's traits are not for the students — who shd be brought patiently to the stage where they may profitably develop their own!

PLATE 42
Writing by Mr Lewis Trethewey

New York, 21 Nov. 1973

Dear Fred:

The western world's taste
may not be beyond redemption,
even if our present conversion to italic
handwriting is still incomplete. In
the U·S·A; acceptance has come
from enough primary & secondary
schools, and from art schools &
colleges, to have trained up a corps of
instructors for that happier day
when italic's promised 'restauration'
shall have made a prophet of

Vostro gratissimo

Paul Standard

dear Alfred, I feel the joy of handwriting
comes as a moment of truth, when
one forgets the pen, the paper, the
hand, but suddenly is aware of the
words as they magically appear.
this enrichment and reward may
be a long time in coming, but when
it does, one knows.
Best wishes,
            Maury Nemoy

Should handwriting be beautiful as well as clear? There is a danger of self-consciousness in a beautiful script, as in a cultivated style: calligraphy replacing communication. A Handwriting Manual is perhaps the only place where the medium may safely become the message.

Yet in a handwritten document, message and medium subtly affect each other. Objectively, the message should remain unchanged; but its nature affects the care taken by the writer, and the writing in turn dictates the impact of the message on each successive reader. An attempt to write beautifully expresses the writer's hope that the reader may be pleased.

PLATE 45
Writing by Mr Bruce Barker-Benfield

'What pleasure is like the pleasure of pen and ink, when you are in the heart of it', said Elizabeth Barrett Browning. To be remembered : — The Chinese calligrapher Yu, who danced before his emperor when asked to write, 'Then, moistening his long brushes, how he dipped and splashed!'; The 9th Century Irish scribe : 'Pleasant to me is the glittering of the sun upon the margins, because it flickers so'; George Sand, 'enveloped in smoke', her pet starling on her shoulder; Virginia Woolf on a wet Sunday : 'I can't help disporting myself on this free blue page.' She admired the writing of Elizabeth I, 'beautiful and elegant as the marks of the waterfly on smooth waters.' And William Plomer thought Virginia's own hand 'sharp, delicate and rhythmical as her own prose.'

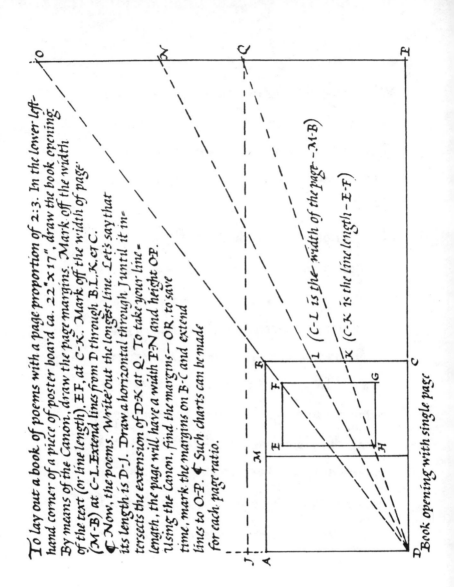

Writing by Professor Lloyd J. Reynolds, Oregon. (Plate 21 of his Italic Calligraphy & Handwriting. *Pentalic Corporation.) 1969*

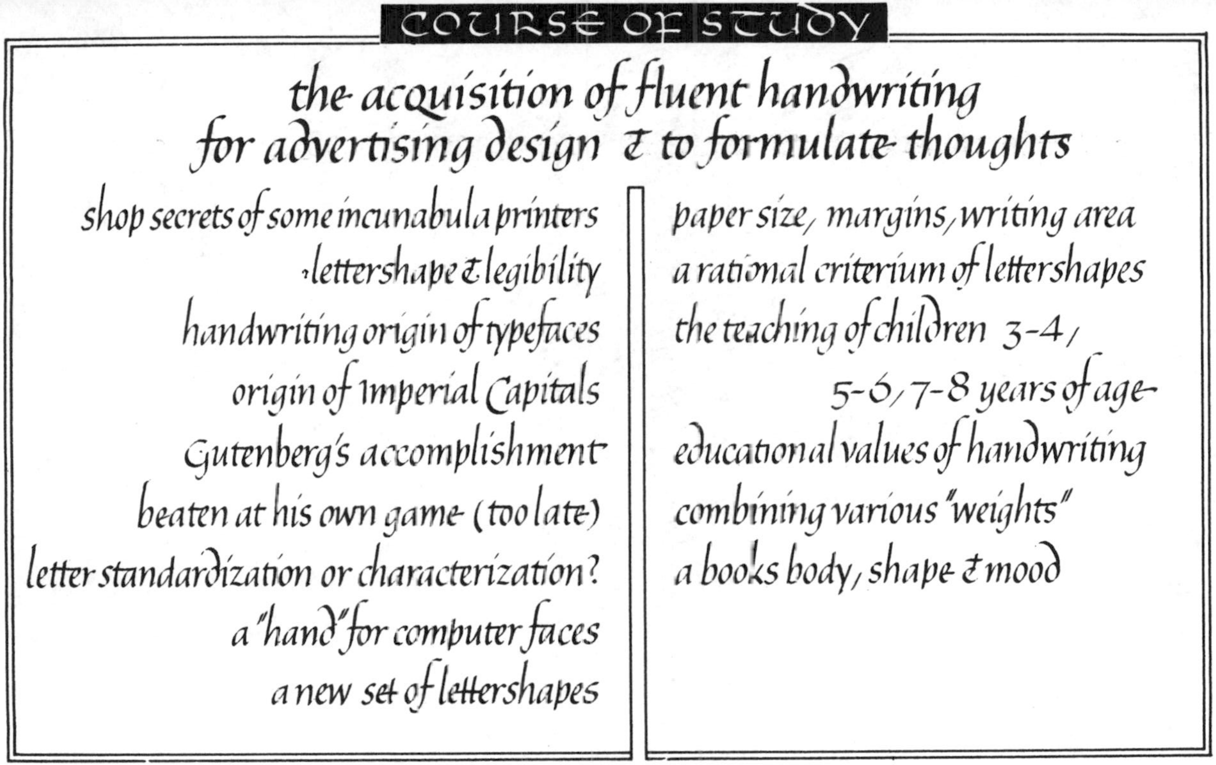

the acquisition of fluent handwriting
for advertising design & to formulate thoughts

shop secrets of some incunabula printers
lettershape & legibility
handwriting origin of typefaces
origin of Imperial Capitals
Gutenberg's accomplishment
beaten at his own game (too late)
letter standardization or characterization?
a "hand" for computer faces
a new set of lettershapes

paper size, margins, writing area
a rational criterium of lettershapes
the teaching of children 3-4,
5-6, 7-8 years of age-
educational values of handwriting
combining various "weights"
a books body, shape & mood

PLATE 48

Writing by Mr Alf Ebsen, Ontario. (Reduced in size)

Dear Mr. Fairbank

Layout, it seems to me, is almost as important an ingredient in good letter writing as the quality of the hand itself.

Without some thought having been given to the arrangement of the component parts of the letter... the address, date, salutation message, close and signature, even a beautiful hand will tend to look undistinguished. Conversely, an ordinary hand with proper layout will produce a letter with a very pleasing aspect. Even a few minutes of extra time given only to maintaining good margins is time well spent.

I sometimes quickly write the outside address several times on a piece of scratch paper before addressing the envelope. Layout, to me, seems well worth the effort.

yours sincerely,
Arthur L. Davies

PLATE 49
Writing by Mr Arthur L. Davies, Colorado

Dear Mr. Fairbank:

After the mastery of the letter forms, the running or cursive element in handwriting is the most important. It keeps the writing from becoming too self conscious and brings grace, style and personality.

Let your hand run as fast as you can while keeping your letters regular and consistant.

Write, as the late Stanley Morison says he wrote, "straight off."

Sincerely yours

James Hayes

PLATE 50
Writing by Mr James Hayes, Colorado

It might prove useful to consider some of the formal & informal aspects of writing. Just as the word implies, formal writing is done slowly & carefully with concern for copybook perfection. Each part of the letter may be done with a separate stroke. The resulting letters tend to be quite stiff. Informal writing employs as few strokes as possible. Very informal writing becomes a personal script. Joins are used to facilitate speed. Italic seems the only letter form suitable for such informal purposes. It remains legible despite the joins & speed.

PLATE 51
Writing by Mrs Jacqueline Svaren, Oregon

Children use writing as one of the means of learning, and in America they generally begin with a print script, later changing to a commercial cursive. Often the change results in a great deal of frustration due to the lack of continuity in letterforms. Fortunately, Italic provides a legible, graceful and individual alphabet that can be written easily yet beautifully by children and adults. Hopefully more and more schools will adopt Italic as the basic script – bringing a lifetime of pleasure to those who write.

PLATE 52
Writing by Mrs Barbara Getty, Oregon

(Dear Mr. Fairbank,

It is encouraging to learn that a new edition of your manual is being prepared. It seems to suggest that you have the support of a "silent majority" who, in spite of the influences of technology, are still in favour of acquiring a good hand.

It is the humanizing aspect of handwriting which will ensure it's survival, & I trust your book will continue to establish all that is best in this basic skill.

Yours sincerely, T. B.

PLATE 53
Writing by Mr Thomas Barnard. (Reduced in size)

SUBJECT INDEX OF TEXT

(Plates, where referred to, are shown in bold type)

143

Subject Index of Text